THE **AUDUBON SOCIETY** GUIDE TO

# Nature Photography

*Impala, Nairobi National Park, Kenya*

# THE AUDUBON SOCIETY GUIDE TO
# Nature Photography

# Tim Fitzharris

Stoddart

Published in Canada in 1990 by
Stoddart Publishing Co. Limited
34 Lesmill Road
Toronto, Canada
M3B 2T6

Published in the United States by
Little, Brown and Company
34 Beacon Street
Boston Massachusetts
02108 U.S.A.

Canadian Cataloguing in Publication Data

Fitzharris, Tim, 1948-
    The Audubon Society Guide to Nature Photography

ISBN 0-7737-2407-9

1. Nature photography.   I. Title

TR721.F57 1990       778.9'3 — dc20       C90-093363-1

Printed and bound in Singapore

*Daisies and red poppies, Italy*

To Lisa

Books by Tim Fitzharris
*The Island*
*The Wild Prairie*
*The Adventure of Nature Photography*
*British Columbia Wild*
*Wildflowers of Canada* with Audrey Fraggalosch
*Canada: A Natural History* with John Livingston
*American Birds*

*Moose in snowsquall, Montana*

*Great white heron, laughing gulls, and double-crested cormorants, Florida*

The NATIONAL AUDUBON SOCIETY, incorporated in 1905, is one of the oldest and largest conservation organizations in the world. Named after American wildlife artist and naturalist John James Audubon, the Society has nearly 600,000 members in 500 chapters, nine regional and five state offices, as well as a government affairs center in Washington, D.C. Its headquarters are in New York City.

The Society works on behalf of our natural heritage through scientific research, environmental education, and conservation action. It maintains a network of almost 90 wildlife sanctuaries nationwide and conducts ecology camps for adults and a youth program for school children. The Society publishes the leading conservation and nature magazine, *Audubon*, and an ornithological journal, *American Birds*, and produces *World of Audubon* television specials, newsletters, video cassettes and interactive discs, and other educational materials.

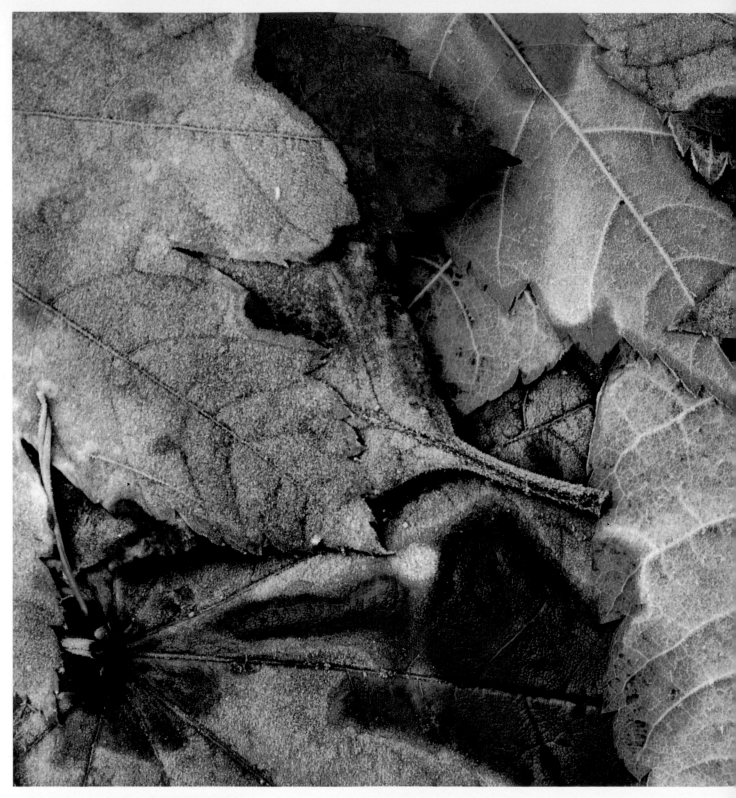

*Vine maple leaves, Coast Mountains, British Columbia*

# CONTENTS

Earthling. A simple word that expresses the common reality we share with all the organisms that live on this planet. The earth is home to us as well as to the elephant, the shrew, and the sycamore tree. We are neighbors and relatives. Yesterday our ancestors swam in the same seas and, if we are lucky, tomorrow our progeny will bask under a common sun.

Although human history records our insatiable drive to monopolize the material resources of the planet, we nevertheless share a spiritual bond with other earth species. This link is evident each time we scratch a dog's ear, listen to a spring robin, or cast our eyes up into the spreading limbs of an oak. The energy that binds all earthly life transcends issues of disappearing rainforests or third world debt.

Nature photography is a channel through which we can better know and appreciate this spiritual link. The camera, like the painter's brush or the poet's pen, is a tool we can use to explore our planet. With it we can peer into the feathers of a snipe or feel the colors of a pine forest. We can sit side by side with the woodchuck or run with the wolf. We can coax the unfolding daisy or sigh with the stars and moon. And if we can look through the lens with eyes wide open, we may be rewarded with a picture of our own soul.

*Arctic fox, St. Paul Island, Alaska*

13

# Chapter One

# Beginnings

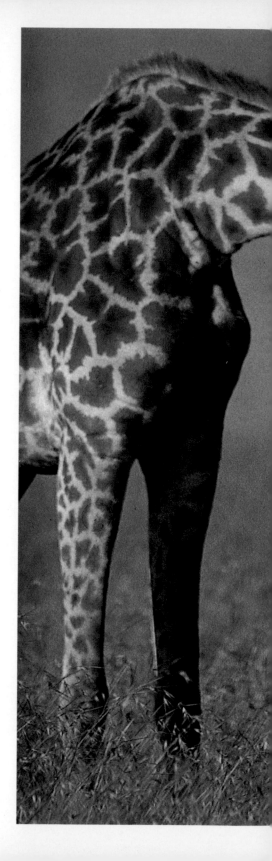

Cameras are simple machines that make recordings of reflected light on film. If you were to remove all of the camera's knobs, levers, and dials a small, light-tight box would remain. The film is positioned at one end of this box. At the other end is a lens that gathers light and directs it onto the film.

Operating a camera is easy. It involves controlling the amount of light that enters the box and focusing this light precisely on the film. Most of the camera's mechanical functions serve these purposes in one way or another. There are many different types of cameras. Usually they are classified by the size of the film used and the design of the viewing system.

Rangefinder cameras, such as popular instamatic varieties, have a viewing system that is separate from the lens that directs the light to the film. As a result the photographer's view of the subject is slightly different from what the film actually records. This disparity increases as the camera-to-subject distance decreases, making accurate framing difficult, if not impossible. Rangefinder cameras therefore are not suitable for small subjects like wildflowers or close-ups of larger subjects such as giraffes.

Unlike the rangefinder camera, a view camera allows you to see the exact image that will be recorded on the film. The scene is viewed on a semi-transparent ground glass that is subsequently replaced by the film and film holder

**GIRAFFE CALF AND MOTHER:** *Fast-handling equipment permitted me to record the brief moment when this young giraffe, still totally dependent on its mother, seems to have assumed the dominant role. Modern cameras greatly simplify the picture-making process. Most have large, bright viewfinders, built-in light meters, and interchangeable lenses. Some offer automatic film loading, automatic exposure, or even automatic focusing. These convenient features free you from many of photography's technical concerns, and like other artists, you can direct your attention to the substance of your message rather than to the question of how it can be delivered.*

before the exposure is made. To make viewing easier the photographer shrouds himself in a black cloth to eliminate reflections on the ground glass. View cameras are large and heavy, making them unwieldy in the field. They must be reloaded after each exposure, so rapid shooting is impossible. Although the viewfinder is accurate, the scene is upside down and reversed, making it difficult to frame moving subjects. View cameras are used in nature photography primarily for making detailed pictures of landscapes where there is plenty of time to compose the scene.

### THE IDEAL CAMERA
The single-lens reflex (SLR) camera is used by most serious nature photographers. The scene is viewed directly through the lens by means of a short periscope (called a pentaprism) that provides an accurate, right-side-up image. Just prior to exposure, a mirror that reflects the image up through the pentaprism to your eye swings out of the way, allowing the light to strike the film directly. This happens in the blink of an eye so that pictures can be taken continuously without losing track of the subject.

Single-lens reflex cameras commonly use 35 mm size film, but larger formats are available. These cameras (made by Hasselblad, Rollei, and others) are difficult to carry in the field and generally are used for studio work. Most published nature photographs are made with a 35 mm SLR camera. This type of camera has a number of advantages in addition

to its accurate viewing system and portability.
* It operates quickly so that photography of wildlife and other active subjects is possible.
* The camera body is the nucleus for an extensive system of accessories including interchangeable lenses, motor drives, and close-up attachments that make it suitable for all subjects.
* Many high quality, relatively inexpensive films are available.

### Buying a 35 mm Single-lens Reflex Camera
There are many brands and models of interchangeable-lens 35 mm SLRs on the market and choosing one may seem difficult at first. Buy a well-known brand such as Nikon, Canon, or Minolta. These companies provide good service and an extensive selection of lenses and other accessories for their cameras.

Whether the camera has manual or automatic exposure is not important. Just be sure, should you buy an auto-exposure type, that

*FERRUGINOUS HAWK LANDING AT THE NEST: The 35 mm SLR camera is ideal for photographing active subjects like this hawk and its nestlings. The camera was attached to a tripod-mounted 500 mm telephoto lens enabling me to work at a distance that did not alarm the birds. When the adult landed I took pictures at five frames per second with the help of a motor drive attached to the camera. One of the shots caught the hawk with its wings in this classic position. Because 35 mm film is relatively inexpensive, I didn't mind shooting a few extra frames, especially of such an uncommon subject. Ferruginous hawks are a threatened species.*

**COYOTE AMONG PRICKLY PEAR CACTUS:** *After a few days of camping in Arizona's Sonoran Desert, I realized that a coyote made a tour of the site every day around lunchtime. One day I set up the tripod and camera with a 700 mm lens near my tent and waited. The coyote showed up on schedule, and I photographed him as he made the rounds. Automatic, spot-metered exposure kept the coyote properly exposed as he moved in and out of the shadows. Although sunny midday lighting produces pictures with excessive contrast (under-exposed shadows and over-exposed highlights), the shallow depth of field of this picture softens the contrast in the out-of-focus area.*

you can make manual exposures when necessary. Totally manual cameras are becoming scarce, but you will find them easier to use than many of the auto-exposure types, which offer a bewildering array of exposure options, most of which are unnecessary for nature photography. Like other professional photographers, I have auto-exposure cameras, which I use in the manual exposure mode.

Auto-focusing will likely be your next consideration. Like auto-exposure, it's not an important option. Just be sure that you can focus manually whenever you choose. Automatic focusing is advantageous for photographing fast-moving subjects and if this kind of photography appeals to you, you may wish to take a serious look at the auto-focusing models. All of the pictures in this book were taken with manual focus cameras.

An essential feature, often missing on auto-exposure cameras, is depth of field preview. This allows you to view the relative sharpness of the various parts of the scene before exposure. Complete control of composition is not possible without it.

A camera that satisfies these few conditions will be easy to operate and capable of producing pictures of the highest caliber. There are other important features that I have not mentioned but the rest will be incorporated on any interchangeable-lens 35 mm SLR.

Not necessary, but useful, is automatic film advance, an accessory that is built into many recent camera models. With some cameras,

motor drives and winders can be added later. Automatic film winding is most helpful when shooting action or doing extreme close-up work when manual film winding may disturb the precision framing that these pictures require.

Another valuable, but not essential, feature permits the interchange of focusing screens. Slow lenses, or lenses used with close-up accessories or teleconverters, cause the central portion of the standard focusing screen to black out. Special screens, which eliminate such problems, can be inserted to make viewing the scene more accurate.

### The Photographer's Best Friend

The first accessory you should buy is a tripod. It will prevent the camera from moving during exposures and enable you to take the sharpest, most detailed pictures possible. During the exciting light of dawn, dusk, and after dark, exposure times are too long to handhold the camera; a tripod is essential. It is also necessary in doing telephoto or close-up work when camera steadiness is especially crucial to prevent blurring. From an artistic standpoint, a tripod causes you to be more deliberate and thoughtful about setting exposures and composing pictures.

You will be using your tripod a lot and it is best to buy one of good quality. Consider spending at least as much as you would for a telephoto lens. Try to buy a tripod with these features:

* legs of non-corroding, tubular aluminum

provides both tactical and creative benefits. A lens's most evident property is the degree to which it magnifies the subject. With a telephoto lens you can make a detailed portrait of a bird at a distance that doesn't frighten it away. A wide-angle lens allows you to frame a mountain panorama without backing off the edge of a cliff. More exciting is that a variety of lenses expands the range of creative approaches, especially in the treatment of perspective. When taking a picture, select a lens based on how it renders perspective rather than its magnifying power if the latter can be controlled by changing the camera-to-subject distance.

Lenses are classified according to focal length and maximum aperture size. Focal length, the most important characteristic, tells how much the subject will be magnified. A normal 50 mm lens approximates the view of the human eye. Focal lengths have direct

for strength and light weight
* legs without braces for easy set-up of the camera on uneven ground
* lever or clip-lock legs that do not get easily jammed with grit and dust
* an extended height that brings the camera at least to eye level
* a ball and socket head with a quick release shoe.

An inexpensive tripod popular with nature photographers that satisfies all these conditions is the Bogen tripod 3021 with Bogen ball head 3055. I have used this combination for the last five years and find it satisfactory. The head incorporates a quick release shoe, which lets you attach and detach the camera quickly.

Bogen also offers many accessories, including a clamp that allows repositioning the head on one of the legs to make low level shooting, of wildflowers, for example, convenient. Gitzo tripods, also popular with nature photographers, are heavier and more expensive, and their legs have locking collars that jam.

## LENSES

When light strikes an object, it reflects in all directions. The lens is designed to collect and form these light rays into a coherent image on film in the same way the lens of the eye directs light onto the retina.

A camera that uses interchangeable lenses

*PREPARING FOR SUNRISE: With tripods and cameras ready, photographers await sunrise over the Camargue marshes in southern France. To capture the often fleeting drama of dawn and dusk, advance preparation is necessary.*

*NEWFOUNDLAND SHORELINE: A tripod is essential when photographing at twilight because the low light conditions require long exposures — for this scene a shutter speed of 1/2 second. I used an 80-200 mm zoom lens, which allows precise framing adjustments without moving the tripod. The view concentrates on a few simple elements, thereby emphasizing the interplay of color and texture.*

mathematical relationships. A 100 mm lens magnifies the subject twice as much as a 50 mm lens and a 25 mm lens will show the subject only one half as large.

The maximum aperture size of the lens is important because it indicates how much light can be transmitted to the film during exposure. Aperture size is expressed as an inverse of the lens focal length and is called an f number or an f stop. An aperture of f/4.0 has a diameter one fourth of the lens focal length, an aperture of f/3.0 has a diameter one third of the lens focal length. It's enough to remember that large apertures are designated by small f stop numbers and vice versa.

Lenses are frequently described as either 'fast' or 'slow.' These terms refer to the relative duration of the exposure time characteristic of the lens. A lens with a large maximum

**POLYCHROME PASS, ALASKA:** *This scene from Denali National Park was photographed with a normal lens. Even though this focal length renders a field of view very similar to the human eye, the photographer is able to control its impact by framing only those elements of the scene which best communicate his reaction or his intended message. Here the choice of camera angle was an important factor in expressing the great expanse of uninhabited wilderness that characterizes this park. The wildflowers and rocks in the foreground provide a scale against which the viewer can measure the distinctly receding landforms. The eye moves over the foreground, across the lowland tundra, up through the mountain foothills, and finally to the most distant ranges. Each new visual plane encountered is a reminder of the distance travelled.*

aperture is a fast lens because it permits fast or brief exposures. Slow lenses are the opposite.

### The Normal Lens

The normal lens has a focal length of 50 mm. It has about the same angle of view as the human eye. The strength of a photograph made with a normal lens is derived from the essential appeal of the scene itself and the photographer's personal approach. In contrast a picture made with a telephoto or wide-angle lens attains some distinction by the way perspective is distorted. There are no such optical enhancements or distractions in a photograph made with a normal lens.

The normal lens is especially useful in photographing still life such as landscapes, trees, and wildflowers. It is ideal for close-up work when used in combination with suitable accessories. When the beauty of a scene is self-evident, the normal lens is often the most appropriate focal length. It gives the closest representation of what the naked eye sees.

### The Wide-angle Lens

With a focal length of less than 50 mm, the wide-angle lens enables the photographer to work close to the subject and still get all of it in the frame. Aside from such tactical considerations, the wide-angle's value lies in the way perspective is rendered. It creates an impression of expanded depth. Near objects seem closer and distant objects seem farther away than when perceived by the eye. A close-up of an animal will show much more of the

background than an equally magnified image made with a longer focal length. The wide-angle is useful in showing relationships between the subject and its environment.

When using a wide-angle lens focusing should be done carefully because at first glance in the viewfinder the entire scene seems to be sharp due to the optical characteristics of the lens. Even small errors, however, will become evident when the film is enlarged. You should also take care when vertical lines or shapes (such as trees) are part of the scene. They will seem to lean together or apart if the film plane (the camera back) is not kept parallel to them. To change the composition without causing distortion, raise or lower the camera rather than tilt it. Special perspective control (PC) lenses, designed primarily for architectural photography, allow correction of leaning verticals without compromising the way the scene is framed.

## The Telephoto Lens

With a telephoto lens (focal length over 50 mm) you are able to make detailed, intimate photographs of wildlife at a safe distance. For this kind of work I use a 500 mm lens. It produces ten times more magnification than the normal lens. Even though this sounds powerful, you still must get within 15 or 20 feet of a cottontail or bluejay to make a frame-filling portrait. A telephoto lens of 500 mm or more is large and heavy and requires the use of a sturdy tripod. It doesn't fit into a gadget bag

and usually a photographer doesn't carry one into the field unless he's sure he will use it.

Moderate telephoto lenses (200 to 300 mm) are suitable for larger animals as well as still life subjects when a compressed perspective is desired. A telephoto lens reduces the apparent distance between near and far objects in the scene. Pictures of a meadow with daisies squeezed together in abnormal profusion or a landscape of tightly stacked hills are products of a telephoto lens.

A common technical failing of telephoto photographs is lack of image detail. This is generally caused by movement or vibration of the camera during exposure. In addition to using a tripod, you should trip the shutter using a cable or electric release, or use the camera's self-timer, to avoid jarring the camera with your hands. Keep the lens and

*GLAZED ROCKS NEAR HUDSON BAY: Freezing rain imparts a special texture to these tundra rocks near Churchill, Manitoba. A 24 mm wide-angle lens created an obvious difference in size between the rocks in the foreground and those on the horizon, which exaggerates the depth of the scene. Wide-angle lenses work well with free-form objects like rocks because the distortion of shape does not become apparent as it does with vertically oriented structures like buildings or trees.*

*CLOSE-UP OF A ROADRUNNER: An important consideration when selecting a telephoto lens is its close-focusing ability. The standard close-focusing distance for most lenses is one meter (three feet) for each 100 mm of focal length. The 500 mm lens shown in the photo focuses to five meters. Obviously, the camera-loving roadrunner is too close. I set up this scene by putting a favorite roadrunner snack, chicken livers, inside the lens hood to draw the bird near.*

camera shielded from the wind. Shutter speeds faster than 1/50 second or slower than 1/2 second produce the least camera vibration, and are recommended when sharpness is critical. Some cameras permit the reflex mirror to be locked up prior to exposure, which greatly reduces vibration.

## Special Lenses

* A ZOOM LENS offers a continuous range of focal lengths in one package. It saves weight and space in your gadget bag and reduces the need to change lenses. It allows you to change the magnification of the scene without changing camera positions, a boon especially when shooting landscapes. Modern zoom lenses have good optical quality and are less

**EVENING IN THE SMOKY MOUNTAINS:** *In landscape photography telephoto lenses can be used to magnify and isolate small areas of a scene to emphasize a pattern, texture, or other special feature. Long lenses also have a flattening effect on perspective and make the receding planes of a vista appear stacked together as is evident in this photo made with a 300 mm lens. A two second exposure was chosen to minimize the effect of camera vibration, an important consideration in telephoto photography when fine detail is required. In addition the camera was mounted on a tripod and the shutter was activated with a remote electric release. The effect of atmospheric haze increases with distance, and here it helps to define the separate mountain ranges and to accentuate the rhythmic pattern of the intersecting slopes. The precise framing that this scene required is easily accomplished with a telephoto zoom lens.*

expensive than buying two or three fixed focal length lenses which cover the same range. Many zoom lenses also have close focusing capabilities similar to macro lenses. I use zoom lenses except for situations that call for an extreme telephoto or wide-angle focal length.

* A MACRO LENS differs from standard lenses in that it focuses closer than normal. It is suitable for small objects as well as distant scenes. Macro lenses have fixed focal lengths and relatively small maximum apertures. They are unequaled in producing high quality pictures of flat surfaces, but such subjects are rare in nature photography. There are other satisfactory ways of making close-up photographs that are less expensive and more versatile than using macro lenses.

* AN APO LENS is a lens of special design that reduces optical aberrations common in focal lengths of 400 mm or longer. Such lenses are

*FROZEN RUFFED GROUSE FEATHER AND WILLOW LEAVES: If you take a closer look, an endless source of photographic inspiration can be found on the forest floor and a wide variety of accessories are made to adapt your SLR for close-up work. The most challenging aspect of making close-ups of still life subjects is creating an interesting design. Most photographers take cues from the natural situation. In this picture made with a 100 mm macro lens, the feather and leaves were bonded by the ice and both seemed to be decaying and returning to the earth. To sustain this idea, the feather, the more interesting of the subject elements, was placed in a less prominent position in the composition to prevent it from dominating the general theme.*

expensive, but if you enjoy photographing wildlife, they are worth the extra cost.

\* A TELECONVERTER is an auxiliary lens that multiplies the focal length of a prime lens. A 2x teleconverter will make a 200 mm lens into a 400 mm lens. Unfortunately the longer focal length is two f stops slower. There is also a decrease in image quality. I sometimes use a less powerful 1.4x teleconverter, which multiplies the focal length by 1.4x and reduces the aperture size by one stop, but I am seldom happy with the results.

## The Lenses in Your Gadget Bag

Luckily there isn't an official list of lenses that a nature photographer should have. Ideally you would like to have access to focal lengths from ultra wide-angle to super telephoto. Carrying this much equipment, however, would make you stagger.

Your field bag is best provisioned with a few lenses that are valuable for their versatility or their suitability to your special interests. Two zoom lenses, one a wide-angle to short telephoto and the other a short to moderate telephoto, will cover most picture situations. Zooms with close-up (macro) capability permit intimate photography of small plants and animals without adding additional weight to your gadget bag. In addition to these two lenses you could comfortably take along a fixed telephoto of 300 or 400 mm for shooting wary animals. This may not sound too burdensome, but remember you will also be carrying a tripod, film, filters, a few close-up

**MALE POLYPHEMUS MOTH:** *Inexpensive accessories, such as extension tubes, can be attached to standard lenses to enable them to focus at closer distances. This large moth was photographed with a 50 mm normal lens and an extension tube from a few inches away. To calm the creature, I put him in the refrigerator for a few minutes — a technique that works well and is harmless to cold-blooded animals. Then I carefully placed him on some leaves and photographed him until he warmed up and flew away.*

accessories, a light reflector, binoculars, and your lunch.

It isn't necessary to buy lenses that are manufactured by the maker of your camera if generic types are available. They are less expensive and it is unlikely anyone will ever be able to see a difference in optical quality, should there be one, by examining the pictures that result. From a mechanical standpoint camera brand lenses may stand up better to the rough conditions you experience in the field.

## FIELD ACCESSORIES

Photographers love gadgets, small accessories that make field work more enjoyable or picture making easier to control. I've tried a lot of them and you would likely enjoy doing the same. Here is a list of my favorites.

* PEANUT BUTTER CANISTER. I fill an empty 35 mm film canister with peanut butter. I use the peanut butter to lure shy animals attracted by the smell and taste.

**PARADE OF LESSER FLAMINGOES:** *This close-up view of lesser flamingoes was made with a 500 mm lens and a 1.4x teleconverter, which resulted in an effective focal length of 700 mm. This combination magnified the subject about 14 times. Photographers working with such powerful telephotos who are concerned with sharpness sometimes use two tripods, one under the lens and the other beneath the camera. However, this approach makes it difficult to adjust the framing of the scene. Although not as solid, it seems to be sufficient to mount the lens on a tripod and then attach a small ball and socket head and a monopod to the camera body.*

* SMALL PAINT BRUSH. I clean dust from my lenses and cameras with this.

* FINGERTIPLESS GLOVES. Whenever it gets cold these gloves keep my hands warm and nimble.

* COLLAPSING LIGHT REFLECTOR. I use this accessory (brand name Flexfill), which is made of reflective fabric stretched inside a springy plastic hoop that folds up to 1/3 its size, to control lighting in close-up photography.

* TRIPOD LEG CLAMP. Small but heavy, this clamp lets me remove and reposition the tripod head near the bottom of one of the legs for shooting low-to-the-ground subjects. Made by Bogen.

* ELECTRIC SHUTTER RELEASE. This is important for vibration-free exposures. I use it most of the time with all lenses.

* COMPACT BINOCULARS. These sometimes allow me to evaluate a picture possibility from a distance. They can save a lot of walking and are handy for birdwatching.

* FILTERS. I carry various ones to help control the light. More about filters in the next chapter.

* EXTENSION TUBES. These are attached to the lens for close focusing. More about these in chapter 4.

* TOY MOUSE. Attached to the end of about 30 feet of fishing line, the toy mouse can be tossed into the grass below a sleeping owl and then pulled in. It's my most exotic accessory but nothing perks an owl up faster.

* RAIN SLEEVE. I cut out the ankle to shin

portion of an old pair of rubber stocking waders and when it rains I pull it over the lens and camera and keep shooting. I have a longer one that slips over my camera with 500 mm telephoto attached.

* LENS HOODS. When the sun's position lies anywhere but directly behind the camera there is a chance of stray light entering the lens. This reduces image contrast and color saturation. I use Cokin lens hoods which clip onto my filter holders.

* MINIATURE ALARM CLOCK. When camping I use a digital alarm clock about the size of a lens filter to rouse me for pre-dawn shooting.

CARING FOR EQUIPMENT

Your cameras and lenses will work satisfactorily in the field if you remember to keep them clean and dry. At the end of each day of shooting, dust off your equipment with a small paint brush and wipe it with a cloth. When you change film, examine the chamber for dust and brush it clean if necessary. Try not to touch the shutter curtain. If sand gets into the moving parts, avoid manipulating the mechanism until the camera can be professionally cleaned. Should something jam, check the batteries. Activate other mechanisms that are working; sometimes this will unlock the jam. Don't force anything as this will only result in more expensive repairs.

If you are working in the rain, the camera should be covered with a plastic bag or rubber sheet. Keep a towel handy to wipe off the drops that gather while you are shooting. If you take

*SHATTERED TREES ON THE OREGON DUNES:* When working in environments where sand or dust is a problem, make sure that your equipment is stored tightly in its case when not in use. The wind is strong enough along the Oregon coast to blow sand into a gadget bag left open while you are preoccupied with picture taking. Any accumulated particles should be brushed off immediately. This picture of sand dunes engulfing decaying trees speaks of the ephemeral nature of life. It is visually intriguing due to the strong elements of texture and perspective.

**WHALE PHOTOGRAPHERS:** *Photographing whales in the Gulf of St. Lawrence in Quebec is cold, exhilarating work. There is no reliable way to safeguard equipment when working near saltwater. Water-tight bags and cases can be used to protect equipment in transit, but once you start shooting, cameras and lenses become vulnerable to corrosive saltwater spray and splashes. I keep plastic bags held with rubber bands over cameras and standard size lenses, and slip long rubber sleeves (cut out of old stocking waders) over large telephotos.*

**SURFACING NORTHERN SEA LION POD:** *These sea lions were photographed on the west coast of Vancouver Island near a haul-out site that can be reached by hiking through a rainforest and scampering across a large rock shelf. On the haul-out rocks the mammals are usually sleeping or watching the ocean. You can approach them secretly thanks to the sound of the surf and incoming ocean winds, which keep your scent away from the sea lions. This shot of a group swimming just offshore was made with a 500 mm telephoto.*

your camera from a cold area to a warm area (usually from outside to inside), condensation will form on the surfaces unless you put the camera in a plastic bag.

Should your camera get wet, use any dry heat source (a hair blower) to evaporate moisture, especially that which is hidden from view. Remove the lens and open the back to allow air to enter the interior of the camera. It is better to let the camera heat up somewhat than to leave moisture inside. If the camera is immersed in saltwater, contact your insurance agent.

## Temperature Extremes

The biggest problem when shooting in cold weather is battery failure. Fortunately your own body provides a convenient heat source. Keep the camera inside your coat when not shooting. If the camera must be in the cold for long periods, carry an extra camera body inside your coat and simply switch a warm camera for a cold one when necessary. Some cameras have remote battery packs connected to the camera by a wire that you can keep warm inside your coat. Others have easy-loading battery cassettes that can be switched in and out as necessary. Nickel cadmium batteries provide the most power in cold temperatures.

In dry, sub-freezing weather static electricity may build up inside the film chamber as the film moves across the felt strips that prevent light from entering the cassette. This may cause sparking inside the camera which

registers on the emulsion. At very low temperatures film becomes brittle and may crack if not wound and rewound gently.

At high temperatures camera lubricants become thin enough to run, possibly gumming up delicate mechanisms. Lens elements can separate, and at temperatures over 50 degrees centigrade, bubbles can form in the glass itself. The best precaution for hot climates is to keep your equipment in the shade. Cover black lenses and camera bodies with white tape if they are going to be out in the sun for an extended period.

The realm of photographic equipment is big and exotic. Many photographers never get much beyond its boundaries. They miss the real thrill and satisfaction of photography — the opportunity to explore their own creativity and to describe a personal reality through their pictures.

# Chapter Two

# Light and Film

The process of making a photograph with a strong artistic statement is complex, but not necessarily difficult. The aerodynamic theory that explains the courtship flight of a hummingbird is also complex, but the bird, like the creative photographer, embraces the activity with joy. A photograph is subject, background, color, and shape. It is timing, exposure, perspective, and angle. Moreover, it is the way that all such elements affect one another. Though significant, these components have little substance. They exist only as reflections, a speck of light energy that has been stored carefully on a section of acetate. Inside the little box that is your camera, you are saving light, not walrus or Himalayan foothills. The beauty of your work may spring from the subject or the ingenuity of the design, but it achieves the highest photographic expression when it comes from the beauty of the light.

Light is variable in intensity, color, direction, and texture. A change in light can transform a mundane subject into one of high drama. Once you become aware of the dominating influence of light on creative photography and learn to control it effectively, you will be able to take advantage of its expressive power.

FILM AND EXPOSURE

The intensity of light is important to the photographer, as this determines film

**BIG-LEAF MAPLES IN WINTER:** *I had driven past this jumble of limbs and trunks often without giving it a second look. But one winter day a shaft of sunlight, rare at this time of year on the Washington coast, painted the buds and moss with gold and cast autumn's leftover leaves in bronze. All I had to do was frame the densest part of the grove, dial in f/16 for maximum depth of field, and make sure the lens was shaded from any direct sunlight. The dramatic backlighting, Fujichrome 50, and Mother Nature took care of the rest.*

exposure. Through the course of a day, light intensity changes constantly while the sensitivity of any given film remains the same. By adjusting the camera's settings you insure that the film will be properly exposed.

Correct exposure is achieved by controlling both the intensity of light that strikes the film and the duration of the exposure. You have the option of blasting the film quickly (large aperture/brief shutter speed), illuminating it slowly with weak light (small aperture/long shutter speed), or anything in between as long as the amount of light reaching the film remains the same for each exposure.

The intensity of light entering the camera is controlled by the size of the aperture. Each aperture setting is one-half the size of the next larger one. These settings, called f stops, are commonly calibrated as f/2, f/2.8, f/4, f/5.6, f/8, f/11, f/16, etc. with f/16 representing the smallest aperture. Some lenses have a wider range of stops.

The duration of the exposure is controlled by the shutter. Exposure times are calibrated so that each is halved with every increase of the shutter speed. Standard shutter speeds in seconds are 1, 1/2, 1/4, 1/8, 1/15, 1/30, 1/60, 1/125, 1/500, and 1/1000 with many cameras offering a wider range of speeds.

In order to set the aperture and shutter speed you must first measure the ambient light. This is easy because all 35 mm SLR

cameras have built-in light meters. You simply compose the scene, turn on the light meter, and it indicates a combination of f stop and shutter speed that will produce a correct exposure. You then make the corresponding adjustments to the settings. With an auto-exposure camera this is done for you.

Once an exposure is indicated, it is a simple procedure to move to a new combination of aperture and shutter speed that may be more suitable to the subject. Suppose the meter calls for a speed of 1/60 second, but you would prefer to shoot three stops faster at 1/500 second to freeze the motion of a bird in flight. This new shutter speed lets in less light, and to compensate for the loss, you increase the aperture size by a corresponding three stops. This retains the exposure indicated by the light meter. With an auto-exposure camera, the aperture would automatically open up the necessary amount when you dialed in the new shutter speed. With a little practice, manipulating f stops and shutter speeds

**WILLET TAKING OFF:** *Arresting the motion of this shorebird required a shutter speed of 1/750 second. When photographing active subjects with a telephoto lens, I use a medium speed film (ISO 50 to 100) and set the lens at maximum aperture. This allows the fastest shutter speed possible under all lighting conditions. Just prior to launch, willets flex their legs to hop out of the water — a clue that assists with the critical timing of the shutter release.*

**POLAR BEARS WRESTLING ON THE SHORES OF HUDSON BAY:** *If the exposure reading of the camera's light meter had been followed, the white bears and bright snow would have been under-exposed since the meter interprets all scenes as average. To retain the natural color of snow scenes, you can increase exposure by one or two stops from the meter reading, or for more accuracy, make a close-up reading of part of the scene that is of average brilliance. For these photographs I used spot-meter readings from the rock rubble seen in the foreground of the smaller picture. In November polar bears gather on the shores of Hudson Bay near Churchill, Manitoba, waiting for the ice to form so that they can venture out to hunt seals.*

40

while retaining correct exposure is easy.

## Exposure Basics

Due to the changing nature of sunlight and the variety of ways that subjects reflect it, attaining satisfactory exposures is sometimes tricky. It helps to understand how the light meter and film work together.

Film is manufactured in a wide range of light sensitivities. There are 'fast' films (more sensitive) and 'slow' films (less sensitive). The light sensitivity of a film is designated by an 'ISO' number, the smaller the number the less sensitive the film. Nature photographers commonly use films between ISO 25 and ISO 200. Slow films produce more detailed photographs with better color but their usefulness is limited in dim light.

If you remember that a light meter interprets every scene as if it were average, you will quickly master film exposure. If the scene is of average brilliance — a mixture of various colors and no dominance of dark or light hues — then you simply follow the meter recommendation and a perfect exposure should result.

Exposure problems develop when the subject is not average. A scene dominated by bright snow is a common example. Keep in mind that the meter can only measure light; it cannot distinguish a snow field from a coal field, and it always indicates settings for an average scene. If you were to follow the meter, the snow would be reproduced as an average middle gray, not a brilliant white.

When you understand the straight-jacket thinking of your light meter you can easily compensate for its failings. In order to retain the snow's brilliance, you simply give the film more exposure than the light meter calls for, usually one or two stops is satisfactory in such a case. When a subject is unusually dark, you simply reverse the procedure, giving less exposure than the meter calls for.

In order to accurately interpret your light meter readings, you must know how it measures the light. Some meters give an integrated reading of light from the entire scene (averaging meter), others measure only a small, clearly defined spot (spot meter), and the most popular type uses a center-weighted system that gives priority to the center of the frame but also measures the light from the rest of the field (center-weighted meter). Some auto-exposure cameras incorporate all three methods and you choose the one most appropriate to the scene. Any of these is satisfactory, but with experience you will come to prefer the spot meter. It allows you to make precise readings of small parts of the scene for which you may wish to give exposure priority because of their importance to the composition.

## The Limitation of Film

Film is able to record only a portion of the range of light intensity that our eyes can. On a clear, sunny day there is great contrast

41

between the lightest and darkest parts of a scene. Our eyes are able to see all the details whether they are in shadow or lit brightly by the sun. But film, especially color transparency film, the nature photographer's favorite, is sensitive only to one or the other. If you set the exposure for the shadow areas, they will be satisfactorily recorded, but the brightest areas, the highlights, will be over-exposed and lack detail. The reverse would be true if you were to give priority to the highlights. On overcast days the light is more even, and shadows and highlights fall within a range the film can register simultaneously.

High contrast is usually caused by the nature of the light source, but a subject can have high contrast as well if it is composed of dark and light tones. A zebra is an extreme example. In addition some films produce more contrast than others. A nightmare for photographers would be to shoot a ski race between polar bears and black bears on a sunny day at noon with a high speed transparency film. Controlling contrast is a major factor in making high quality images and it will be discussed more in subsequent sections.

## Practical Exposure Tips

* LEARN THE f/16 RULE. It enables you to easily determine correct outdoor exposure without a light meter. It can be an even more reliable way of determining exposure than taking meter readings, and it is useful to check the accuracy of your meter. During the middle part of a sunny day, you simply set the aperture at f/16 and the shutter at the inverse of the film speed. If you are using Kodachrome 64 (ISO 64), the shutter speed should be set at 1/60 second, the closest speed to 64. Change to a faster or slower shutter speed if you like, just be sure to compensate with the necessary adjustment of the aperture.

* LOOK FOR A MID-TONE. Knowing that your light meter works best on average subjects, take a close-up reading of such an area in the scene if it is a high contrast situation. This is easily done with spot metering. If you're using an averaging meter, move closer to fill as much of the frame as possible with the mid-tone while you make the reading. Use this reading as the basis for the exposure. If the scene has no middle tone, meter something close by that does. Just be sure that it is in the same light and that the lens focus remains unchanged from your intended target. The

**BONAPARTE'S GULL PREENING:** *A conventional meter reading would have misinterpreted this scene, due to the large expanse of black in the composition. Programmed for average subjects, the meter would have indicated an exposure that rendered the water as a mid-tone gray and over-exposed the Bonaparte's gull, the most important part of the scene. The darkness of the water results from the sun's position just above the horizon — high enough to illuminate the bird but not high enough to create reflections in the water or light up the gravel bar the bird is standing on. The touch of red on the gull's leg accentuates the general absence of color in this composition — essentially a study in black and white.*

**LEAVES IN A PENNSYLVANIA STREAM:** Kodachrome 25, the slide film used for this picture, is fine-grained and produces excellent detail, but compared with other films it reacts slowly to light. This latter characteristic was not a handicap in this situation because the scene was quite still. Even at a shutter speed of 1/2 second there was no blurring of the subject.

clear north sky is a good mid-tone region to meter. In a pinch, meter the palm of your hand and then open up one stop to compensate for the fact that a palm is about twice as bright as the average subject.

* BRACKET IMPORTANT SHOTS. When confronted with a tricky lighting situation you can bracket exposures. This is a systematic process of taking some extra pictures at different exposures in case of mistake. Usually it is sufficient to vary the base exposure by one stop over and one stop under.

## Choosing a Film

Black and white film is used by very few nature photographers today. It cannot come close to communicating the drama or sensuality of color films. Humans see the world in color. It is the most exciting component of our most valued sense and few of us can resist its magic.

Color transparency (slide) film is most popular with nature photographers. It produces images with finer detail and richer, more accurate color than print film. In addition, slides can be projected for an audience or made into sharp, brilliant prints. Slide film is relatively inexpensive, an important consideration if you are shooting fast action and find it necessary to take extra insurance shots. Deciding on which transparency film to use depends on the kind of image you want. Magazines such as *Popular*

*Photography* and *Outdoor Photographer* regularly publish comparative test reports on film, making it easy for you to become familiar with the unique characteristics of different brands.

* SLOW FILM has an ISO rating of around 25. It produces fine-grained, detailed pictures with good color saturation. In this department Kodachrome 25 is unchallenged. It produces the highest quality images of any film. Its lack of speed makes it unsuitable for use in low light situations.

* MEDIUM SPEED FILM is in the 50 to 100 ISO range. It is a compromise between the high quality of slower films and the convenience and speed of faster ones. Kodachrome 64 was long the acknowledged leader in this field but it is now rivaled by Fujichrome 50 and Fujichrome 100.

* FAST FILM (ISO 200 and more) is designed for shooting under low lighting conditions such as those encountered on overcast days

**CROONING ARCTIC FOX:** *On the Pribilof Islands in the Bering Sea, arctic foxes have charcoal-colored fur, which camouflages them on the boulder beaches where they hunt seabirds and forage for carrion. Because of the overcast conditions and the subject's dark color, I used a high speed film (Fujichrome 400). Light levels were further reduced by the location of the fox den in the shadows at the base of an overhanging cliff. A shutter speed of 1/15 second at the lens's maximum aperture of f/4 was necessary. The exposure was not brief enough to arrest the fox's movements, which resulted in an eerie glow about its mouth.*

and at dawn or dusk. It is also valuable when a fast shutter speed is needed to freeze action. For this extra speed, however, you sacrifice the fine grain and saturated color of slower films. Fast film is high in contrast. On sunny days it produces pictures with either washed out highlights or blocked up shadows depending on the choice of exposure. But in soft, overcast light it makes the details of a scene pop out with attractive, contrasting highlights. There is no acknowledged leader in the fast film category. Choosing one is usually a matter of color preference, and even here there is little to distinguish them.

## Storing Film

In order to prevent your transparencies from deteriorating, they should be kept in a cool, dark, dry place. Most picture agencies and professional photographers store their slides in see-through vinyl sheets that hold 20 slides each. This makes it easy to locate a specific picture quickly. Be sure to use archival quality sheets; other kinds emit gases that react adversely with the film emulsion. The sheets can be stored in a normal filing cabinet along with a sock full of silica gel crystals, a drying agent that keeps humidity in the cabinet low, preventing fungus from growing on the slide emulsions.

I keep my slides organized in alphabetical order by subject. As I accumulate more pictures of a certain subject, I break the file down into more manageable portions. For example, when I first started nature photog-

graphy, I had one file entitled 'birds.' Soon I had to divide this file into 'land birds' and 'water birds.' Then I had to divide 'water birds' into 'herons,' 'ducks and geese,' 'sandpipers, gulls, and terns,' and so on. The advantage of this system is that it grows in step with your slide collection, and keeps tedious filing to a minimum.

If you send slides away for publication, each picture should be slipped into a Kimac slide protector, which prevents a slide from being damaged when it is out of the vinyl sheet.

## USING FILTERS

Because the nature photographer's approach is defined in part by the subject matter, the range of filters normally used is small. Filters that would distort or alter the visual concept from that which naturally occurs are rarely used. They usually function to control the contrast of a scene or enhance or balance color.

\* POLARIZING FILTER. I use this filter so much that I keep one attached to my lenses all the time. It reduces or eliminates reflected glare from non-metallic surfaces like leaves, grass, and water, making it especially valuable in producing landscape scenes with saturated color. It will also darken blue skies dramatically when photographed at a right angle to the sun. This filter is adjustable, allowing you to control the amount of reflection by viewing the scene through the viewfinder. It reduces the light reaching the film by one to two stops.

**YUKON TUNDRA IN AUTUMN:** *The leaves of kinnikinnick and huckleberry turn scarlet during August, washing the uninhabited tundra with vivid color as far as the eye can see. In this photo a polarizing filter was used to eliminate reflections from the leaf surfaces, allowing the rich color to register on film. To record the foliage detail, I used a fine-grained film (Fujichrome 50), mounted the camera on a tripod, and shot at an aperture of f/16, which produced a depth of field that extended from foreground to background.*

When buying a polarizing filter, check that it does not cut off the corners of the frame (called vignetting) due to its thickness. This may happen with wide-angle lenses and it can be tested by simply stopping down the lens to smallest aperture and viewing a strong light source with the filter attached. Also be sure that the filter is compatible with the camera's light meter. Some meters require the use of a circular polarizer for correct readings.

* WARMING FILTER. This amber-tinted, series 81 filter is used primarily to enhance warm colors (yellow, orange, red). The warming filter also counteracts the blue cast that appears when subjects are in the shade and illuminated by light from a blue sky. Most photographers use an 81a (least effect) or 81b (moderate effect), which warm up the scene without creating a noticeable color shift. I use these filters frequently when photographing subjects that are dominated by warm color, especially autumn foliage and sunsets.

* GRADUATED NEUTRAL DENSITY FILTER. This is the landscape photographer's best friend. Half of the filter is clear and the other half is neutral density (gray), which filters out all wave lengths of light usually by two or three stops. It is used most often in high contrast landscape work in situations where the sky is much brighter than the land (a usual occurrence). The filter, mounted in a special holder, slides up and down in front of the lens so that the dark part can be positioned against the lightest area of the scene, thereby bringing the luminosity of both the land and the sky

**CANADA GEESE ON THE WING:** *This image is a composite of two separate slides sandwiched together. The color of the background sunset shot was enhanced by the use of an amber-colored warming filter. The shot of the silhouetted geese was made by photographing the birds against a bright overcast sky. The sky was over-exposed three to four stops to render it white (clear on the emulsion). The contrast was so great that the flying birds appear as black silhouettes. When opportunity permits, I take generic background and silhouette shots that may someday be useful in a sandwich. It is not easy to find two slides that work well together: the background photo should not bleed through the silhouette, the perspective of the two photos must match, and the animal should be portrayed in its customary habitat.*

**ADJUSTABLE FILTER SYSTEM:** *A variety of filtration effects are possible with adjustable filter systems such as Cokin's, which consists of square filters mounted in front of the lens in a special holder. Especially useful is the graduated neutral density filter shown above. It can be moved up and down, or sideways, to reduce the brilliance of selected areas of the scene. If used to reduce the brightness of the sky, as is most often the case, it works best when the horizon is straight and clear of projections. Several filters can be mounted in the holder simultaneously.*

**TWILIGHT ON GEORGIAN BAY:** *This photograph was made about 15 minutes after sundown on a summer's evening. The sky was darkened by using a graduated neutral density filter, which caused the lake and rocks in the foreground to appear brighter and take on a surreal quality. The use of an ultra wide-angle lens (20 mm) adds to the dreamlike mood through its distortion of perspective.*

within an exposure range the film can accommodate. The most popular type is produced by Cokin in two grades of density. You should get both for maximum control of high contrast situations.

* ULTRA-VIOLET FILTER. This filter reduces ultra-violet light or haze which can degrade image detail, especially in pictures taken with a telephoto lens over a great distance. It does not cause any significant loss of over-all light transmission or change in color. A polarizing filter works better at reducing haze if losing a stop or two of light is not a problem.

## LIGHT'S NATURAL DRAMA

The sun's energy powers the photosynthetic process that is the basis of life on earth. It is mother of the green Serengeti and the frost-fired maples of Vermont. The pelican, the whale, and the grasshopper are its grandchildren. For nature photographers, sunlight is the essence of the game.

Most of us are accustomed to the sun's relentless energy and unmindful of its day to day nuances. But tuning in to the subtle variations of light, and how it is reflected or absorbed by our photographic subjects, is the key to making exceptional pictures. A photographer notices the shadows on the underside of a charging rhino.

## Direct Sunlight

On cloudless days the light generated by the sun travels in clean parallel rays. From a couple of hours after sunrise until a couple of hours before sunset, it varies little in intensity. On striking an object it casts abrupt shadows like a spotlight. Highlights are brilliant and the contrast range varies as much as ten f stops, twice the range that color transparency film can record. These are poor conditions for shooting. Not only will much of the scene's detail be lost to excessive contrast, but being daytime creatures, we are accustomed to the effect of this light on our environment and find it undramatic.

Clouds improve the situation. Although direct, overhead sunlight is still the main light source, some of the light is scattered as it passes through clouds and is deflected into the shadow areas to lower contrast and improve color saturation throughout the scene. The more clouds the better. A landscape of snow, sand, or bleached grasses also improves the harshness of direct sunlight, reflecting light back up into the shadows. Except for these situations, direct midday sun should be avoided, even in situations where your intention is to express the bleakness of a landscape. Harsh light does not produce a harsh mood. It will likely fail to illuminate details of the scene critical to your theme.

The photographic appeal of the sun improves the nearer it is to the horizon. Because the rays are penetrating the atmosphere at an angle, they encounter more resistance from particles of air, dust, pollution, and water. The

**ATTWATER'S PRAIRIE-CHICKEN:** *Frontlighting vividly illuminates the colors of the scene. By displaying feathers and sounding a booming mating call, this male prairie-chicken is doing his best to win the favors of a nearby hen. I photographed the birds from a blind erected near the booming ground. To coax the birds closer to the camera, mirrors were set up in front of the displaying males, the reflections intended to simulate a rival suitor. The wads of yellow paper stuck to the mirrors also stimulate the males to display. The paper mimics the prairie-chickens' yellow pouches, which are expanded during the booming and dancing rituals.*

clean parallel rays of high noon are broken up. They lose intensity, which limits the choice of aperture and shutter speed, but at the same time they develop fuzzy edges, making shadows less dense and distinct, bringing the contrast range of the subject closer to the range of the film. The suspended particles also filter the light, absorbing primarily the blue wave lengths and warming the colors of the scene. If this were not enough to tempt you to get up early and retire late, the sun's low position in the sky offers a choice of lighting angles other than just the unflattering overhead position of midday.

In tropical regions this period of attractive light is less extended because the sun rises perpendicular to the horizon. In polar regions during the summer the photographer experiences long periods of daylight, and for a few days the sun will not dip below the horizon at all. Of course this photographic utopia is fleeting, for during the winter, darkness dominates to a comparable extent.

## Frontlighting

If the sun is behind you, it lights up the part of the subject facing the camera. The lower the sun is in the sky the more evenly the scene is illuminated. With the sun just above the horizon, the subject loses all shadows and in the bargain its texture, shape, and depth. This may be very appropriate if you wish to depart from the usual conception of perspective or add an abstract quality to the composition. Using flat lighting in a scene with strong perspective cues (such as receding railroad

tracks) creates an intriguingly dynamic irony, the impression that the scene is expanding and contracting as the eye plays back and forth over the contradictory elements. Due to its direct and even illumination, frontlighting is used generally to present saturated color or emphasize color contrast.

## Sidelighting

Light that illuminates the subject from the side reveals texture and form. If the sun is at right angles to the camera/subject axis, the shadows cast are the longest possible and they reveal the wrinkles, ridges, dimples, and other details of a surface in greatest relief.

Sidelighting creates great tonal variation within the scene. This in turn increases the number of graphic elements in the composition and makes it more complicated and difficult to control. The dramatic effect of sidelighting usually works most effectively when the basic picture elements of line, shape, and texture are kept simple.

Because shadow and highlight areas are nearly equal, sidelighting is high in contrast, especially in dry environments with little dust or pollution. If clouds are present they will reflect and deflect light into the shadow areas. In deciding on an exposure you usually should give priority to the highlights and allow the shadow areas to block up. This is not an arbitrary recommendation. It doesn't surprise us to come across objects that are too dimly lit to view clearly, but this rarely happens in reverse. Over-exposing highlight areas usu-

ally confuses the viewer and leads him to question the technical qualities of the image.

## Backlighting

Like the other types of directional lighting discussed, backlighting varies in degree, and is most extreme when the sun is directly behind the subject. Except for a thin highlight around its periphery, the subject is in shadow. This effect is most dramatic on subjects with indistinct edges, like a musk-ox. When backlit it appears to be surrounded by a thick halo of warm light. When the subject is translucent — the plumes of an egret, a jack rabbit's ears, or a maple leaf — the light projects through, imparting to the subject a luminosity of its own.

Backlighting is the most abstract type of illumination. Because of its high contrast, the film records the scene in a way foreign to the naked eye. If the main subject is backlit and photographed against a bright background that receives exposure priority, it will appear as a dark silhouette. Alternatively you may wish to give exposure priority to the subject by taking a close-up reading of the shaded side that faces the camera. This washes out the highlights and over-exposes the background, and as with silhouettes, the effects are unusual and often pleasing. There may be eight or nine f stops between these two extremes. Judging the results is a subjective process. Sometimes all exposure variations work well, each resulting in a different mood. It's a good idea to bracket extensively and choose the effect

*WHITE-TAILED JACKRABBIT: Sidelighting effectively illuminates the contours and surface texture of this jackrabbit. There seems to be no easy way to photograph these nervous and wary animals. I stalk one jackrabbit after another until I come across one that stays put for a while. Another approach is to drive along country roads where they like to feed. The period just before sundown produces the best opportunities and light. This photograph was shot out of the side door of a van with the camera and tripod set up on the floor, using a 500 mm lens and a 1.4x teleconverter.*

that you prefer after the film is developed.

Photographs made with backlighting often lose quality due to lens flare. This happens when sunlight strikes the lens elements directly and, depending on the angle of the sun, causes a loss of color saturation or the appearance of octagonal hotspots. Flare can be eliminated or reduced by using a lens hood, or by changing the camera angle. As its effect changes with aperture size, the scene should be evaluated at shooting aperture.

## Twilight and Nightlight

When the sun is below the horizon, only the light which emanates from the brightness of the sky is available for photography. This light is many times less intense than normal daylight. Even with high speed films and large apertures, exposure times last from seconds to hours and require the use of a tripod. The brightest periods are when the sun is closest to the horizon — before sunrise and after sunset. As the scene is lit evenly by the entire sky, contrast is very low. Shadows, and thus shapes and textures, are indistinct. The light, being reflected from the blue sky, renders the subject in cool, murky monochromes. Film does not react typically when exposure times exceed a second or two, producing unwanted color shifts and underexposure. You can judge from this that twilight photography has serious drawbacks. There are two situations, however, when it can produce appealing results.

The first is when the composition is based on the use of silhouettes juxtaposed against the sky itself. This process is similar to making silhouettes using backlight directly from the sun. With the twilight situations, however, there is no problem with lens flare and exposure calculation is a simple matter of taking an average reading of the sky itself. In addition, the sky which comprises the background is more colorful at twilight, ranging from warm saturated hues near the horizon to deep blue overhead. By adjusting camera angle and focal length, the photographer can incorporate the entire range of color or work with only a limited range.

The most dramatic twilight situation occurs when there are scattered clouds in the sky. For a brief period when the sun is near the horizon, it illuminates the sides and bottom of the clouds with warm light. The clouds become the dominant light source of the

*MULE DEER ENCOUNTER: From its position directly behind these mule deer, the sun illuminates the translucent parts of the scene — the peripheral hairs around the deer's heads and ears. This halo effect is typical of backlighting and becomes most dramatic when the background is dark, a situation that occurs frequently when the subjects are positioned against a shaded hillside. With the elimination of predators and an increase in suitable habitat, deer in North America have increased significantly in the past century. These two were looking for apple peelings tossed from my kitchen window when the photo was made.*

scene. In addition it is rare for them not to be the most powerful visual element when they appear in the composition. The effects are dramatic and change quickly until total darkness arrives.

## Overcast Light

On clear days you can control light quality primarily by timing shooting sessions to the sun's changing position in the sky. On cloudy days, the light is not affected by the sun's position nearly so much as by the nature and extent of the cloud cover. Although the light is less predictable than on clear days, photography is still mostly a matter of reacting to the varied conditions.

Cloudy skies have much variation, from being still and evenly overcast to filled with cottony, wind-driven cumulus. Smoothly overcast conditions produce soft light, illuminating the subject evenly, without noticeable shadows. This low contrast light allows the film to record the complete range of tones and reproduce the scene with saturated colors. Exposure is easy to determine and changes

*AFTER SUNSET ON SEMIAHMOO BAY, WASHINGTON: At twilight the sky presents a changing array of patterns and colors. In this photo, exposure priority was given to the most important part of the sky, causing elements in the foreground that project above the horizon to become silhouettes. In framing this scene I tried to eliminate the surrounding landforms and build a simple composition based on the bands of color in the sky and on the bay.*

little regardless of where you point the camera. Overcast light is most useful in revealing detail in the subject and for producing clear, legible images of subjects that are complex. It has no drama of its own.

Although an overcast sky creates little contrast in the subject, it is nevertheless the main light source and far brighter than the scene it illuminates. If it is incorporated in the composition itself, in a landscape, for example, it cannot be exposed correctly without underexposing the land. If the land is properly exposed, the sky becomes washed out and detracts attention from the rest of the scene. You can avoid this problem by excluding the sky from the composition altogether or by using a graduated neutral density filter to darken the sky where it appears in the frame.

Darker skies filled with storm clouds bring dullness to the scene, lowering contrast so much that modeling, texture, and perspective suffer. These clouds have visual power and pictorial drama of their own, and being dark, they usually fall within the same brightness range of the land and thus can be incorporated into the composition effectively. The brooding effect of a stormy sky can be emphasized by the use of a low-power, graduated neutral density filter.

## Artificial Light

Electronic flash is the only type of artificial light that is of practical use in nature

**ALPINE MONKEY FLOWERS:** *To reduce contrast when photographing small subjects, I use a Flexfill reflector (shown above) to bounce light into shadow areas. This reflector collapses easily and has a permanent home in my gadget bag. This photograph was made with a 100 mm lens mounted on a bellows, a device that permits close-up focusing. The exposure lasted one second and many of the shots were spoiled by an untimely gust that caused the blooms to blur. As is customary for wildflower photographs, the pictures were made using a tripod and a remote shutter release.*

photography. Balanced for daylight film, its quick but intense flash does not harm plants or animals and seldom causes alarm. The brief duration of the flash (usually less than 1/1000 sec.) freezes all but the fastest action. It allows you to handhold even telephoto lenses without fear of camera shake.

The easiest way to obtain correct flash exposure is with a camera that has automatic through-the-lens (TTL) flash metering. You just need to set the appropriate aperture and the camera and flash work together to produce a proper exposure. This system is accurate for any lens, for close-up work, and for when you are lighting the scene with more than one flash at once. Using a manual flash is less convenient. First you must determine the flash-to-subject distance, then you refer to a calculator dial on the flash which provides the correct aperture setting for a range of film speeds. With a moving subject, the flash-to-subject distance changes, and you must continually re-adjust the aperture. Non-TTL automatic flashes will make compensation for a moving subject, but not for different focal lengths, for close-up accessories, or for when the subject is abnormally bright or dark.

### Lighting Accessories

There are few ways that you can control the character of natural light aside from waiting for the right conditions. You can modify the color of the light by use of the appropriate filter, and you can control contrast in a scene, especially landscapes, with graduated neutral density filters. With smaller subjects that you can shoot at close range, contrast can be improved by using reflectors. This may be a square of matt white cardboard or, for more intense reflection, one that is covered with crumpled aluminum foil. They can be any size, but for convenience most photographers carry ones that fold up and fit into the gadget bag. I carry a commercial reflector, called the Flexfill, that is circular and can be used to either reflect light into the subject or, by placing it between the sun and the subject, diffuse and soften the light. It is very light and folds up neatly.

# Chapter Three

# Picture Design

Nature photographs are made primarily because the activity is fun. The fact that they also bring enjoyment to others is a fortunate by-product. Most photographers get up before dawn to wade through a swamp or struggle up a mountain because they like what they see — so much that they want to express the experience to others through their pictures. Sometimes it happens that a person acquires a camera and the discipline of photography forces him to look at the world more critically. In the process he encounters a new and intriguing kind of visual experience.

Whatever the case, nature photography attains its deepest expression when the photographer's motivation arises from his fascination with the visual environment. Some people are more visually oriented than others. They usually develop a long and satisfying interest in photography and make the most exciting pictures.

No matter how inspired you may be, it is necessary to learn the principles of picture design, or composition, to satisfactorily express yourself through photography. A knowledge of picture design lets you clearly communicate the experiences that you find stimulating.

COMPOSITION
Composition is the way you arrange the elements of a picture, that jumble of

**MALIGNE LAKE REFLECTION, ALBERTA:** *Few scenes are as cliché as a snowcapped mountain reflected in a lake. But the monochromatic colors and lack of perspective cues in this composition result in an abstract study of shape and color rather than a picture postcard. Nature is the inspiration for creativity, but it does not impose rules or conventions on your approach to photography. Society's pressure to conform sometimes makes it difficult to stay in touch with your creative faculties. Try to develop thought patterns that focus on your personal ideas about imagery, rather than considering what others might like to see or what other photographers or artists are producing.*

lines, shapes, and textures that appears in the viewfinder. By giving order to these elements you are able to relate a clear message. Composition is the key that unlocks the emotions of the viewer. It is a universal language that reveals the photographer's message to anyone who can see.

## Dominance

Learning to use the language of composition is hardly more difficult than learning to make a correct exposure. All visual design is based on the premise that some things catch the eye more than others. This is what I call the principle of dominance, the fact that picture elements exhibit visual priority. All compositions are structured on this fundamental principle.

Many compositions are organized around a single, striking element (a visual center of interest). More complex compositions are based on a number of elements working together to create a central theme.

Evaluating the visual importance of picture elements is based on an intuitive sense that renders these kinds of conclusions.

* Red is more attractive than yellow.
* Large draws more attention than small.
* Difference draws more attention than conformity.
* Jagged lines are more striking than curved ones.
* Diagonal lines are more attractive than vertical ones.

* Sharpness is more attractive than blur.
* Rough is more attractive than smooth.
* Light is more attractive than dark.

This list is only a sample of the many visual elements that can be compared and evaluated with a clear consensus because visual perception among humans is similar.

The view that confronts you at the foot of a mountain is not as simple as the examples on this list. The complexity of visual elements more often requires you to compare a curved red line with a jagged yellow one; a gray, diagonal, rough texture with one that is smooth, vertical, and chartreuse. These visual comparatives seem difficult to evaluate when described in words, but our eyes can make such assessments quickly. This evaluation process starts unconsciously as soon as you look in the viewfinder and begin manipulating picture elements by asking your subject to smile or move a little closer to the camera.

Those with little experience in composing photographs evaluate the various picture elements they see in the viewfinder for their emotional or intellectual properties rather than their visual ones. Intent on photographing a mule deer, they do not notice a small pool of light in the background. This is to be expected because the bright spot has no real significance until the film is developed — until the multi-sensory experience of the field is transferred onto a flat, silent sliver of acetate. Then vision becomes the sole frame of reference. The drab deer is scarcely apparent

**DAWN IN THE GREAT RIFT VALLEY:** *Certain parts of this composition attract your attention more than others. Though small, the silhouetted trees along the dark slope in the foreground dominate the other picture elements as a result of their intricate shape. These shapes are repeated less distinctly along the horizontal plane in the background (the wall of the Rift Valley). The visual strength of the hill led me to position it in a corner of the frame where it would be less significant and cause the viewer's attention to leave this subject to consider the unusual way in which space and perspective are presented in the photograph. The repetition of shapes and the use of a single warm hue impart unity to the design.*

*FROZEN RED OAK LEAVES: By framing only parts of these leaves, I shifted the emphasis of this picture from the subject matter to the manner in which the graphic elements are arranged. The variety of texture and the sensory appeal of the ice and frost add another dimension to the composition that strengthens its visual appeal.*

in the vegetation, while the out-of-focus high-light is a brilliant pool that attracts immediate attention.

To avoid such oversights, photographers train themselves to remove the normal labels from elements in a scene and think in graphic terms. The photographer perceives his center of interest — the deer — as nothing more than a rectangular brown shape. To make his message clear, it must become the dominant visual element of the composition. Before making the exposure, he changes the camera position to eliminate the bright highlight from the background, and then examines the field for any other elements that might be more attractive than the brown rectangle.

## Shapes, Lines, and Textures

By removing labels from subject matter, you can more easily analyze its visual power. A clump of grass becomes a series of vertical lines, a badger nothing more than a torpedo shape, a lake an expanse of ripples. Only when you are aware of the visual strength of each picture element can you organize a design that will make your statement clear to the viewer. If you train yourself to see the scene as an arrangement of lines, shapes, and textures, this needed visual objectivity results.

Shape is the basic ingredient of most photographs. A walk in the woods reveals many. Mushroom caps are circles, tree trunks are tubes, poplar leaves are triangles. Many natural shapes can be thought of as free-form variations or combinations of formal geometric shapes. Shapes with sharp corners have the most visual impact, probably because the survival instinct has given us a keen awareness of sharp objects like thorns, fangs, spears, and MX missiles. Keep this in mind when you are organizing the visual priorities of a scene.

Lines are not much less than very thin shapes. In a graphic context we think of them as setting the limits of a space, indicating a direction, or linking different parts of a scene. In some pictures lines have a visual substance of their own but we mostly use them to organize and support other visual elements. In nature they are encountered as a strand of hair, a tree branch, the veins of a leaf, the halo outline of a backlit grizzly, the dotted tracks of a mouse in the snow, the stem of a daisy, or the horizon.

Rough, shiny, silky, bumpy, bristly, slippery, grainy, wrinkled, spongy: a wealth of

**DEAD CEDARS REFLECTED:** Most habitats have unlimited possibilities for exciting compositions. But natural designs usually need to be refined before they are transposed onto film. I realized that the forceful vertical elements of these wizened trunks could be best expressed by tight vertical framing that would incorporate the reflection. The vertical format is not generally used unless it is especially suited to the subject matter. Horizontal framing is more natural because of the side-by-side anatomical arrangement of our eyes, which causes us to view the world with a horizontal orientation. If our eyes were positioned one above the other, vertical paintings and photographs likely would be more common.

*RELAXED GRIZZLY: Although you will likely never feel the texture of a grizzly's fur or muzzle, you get a strong impression of it from this photograph. A picture design that uses texture creates a more immediate experience for the viewer than a design that is restricted to visual elements. Grizzly bears can be easily photographed during August at several Alaska locations where they gather to feed on spawning salmon.*

textures exists in nature. There are fuzzy muzzles, satin sand dunes, and hard rumpled backs of alligators. Texture appeals to our sense of touch, but it is closely allied to vision, more so than any of our other senses. Through experience we develop a strong association between seeing and touching. Our eyes quickly learn from our fingertips what is pleasant to touch and what is not. Although we never stop testing textures by touch, as adults we do most of our feeling with hands in pockets and eyes wide open. By showing texture in a composition you can infuse the picture with a sensation other than just the visual and it becomes more convincing and dynamic.

Color

Color evokes the greatest emotional reaction of any of the visual elements. Its presence significantly influences every design. More often than not, it is this aspect of a scene that induces a nature photographer to stop hiking and set up the camera. Color not only projects a visual force of its own but is also an integral part of every shape, line, and texture that we find in a photograph. Our reaction to color is invariably spontaneous and instinctive. Our conscious manipulation of it in designing pictures is primarily concerned with the manner in which different colors relate to one another.

Each portion of the color spectrum evokes a different emotional response. The most attractive, but not necessarily the most

appealing color, is red. We notice it before any other, perhaps because it is the color of blood, the fluid that sustains life and often foretells death. Red is used for our most important signals — stop lights, fire exits, and danger signs. It is rare for this color to be used effectively in a photograph unless it represents or supports the center of interest.

Red, yellow, and orange are called warm colors. They have more visual power than cool colors — the blues and greens. The appeal of a particular hue not only varies with the individual but with his emotional state. We can be subjective in how we use color in our designs provided we keep in mind the simple relationship between warm and cool colors.

In assessing the relative strength of colors you also need to consider color purity. A color is most powerful when it has not been diluted by either white or black. Color purity is

inherent in the subject matter, but it can also be affected by the intensity and the angle of the illumination. Colors in shadow areas have more black and are less brilliant; in highlight areas they become washed out. Exposure can be manipulated to control color saturation in specific parts of the scene.

The strength of a color is greatly determined by its relationship to other colors in the picture. Colors gain apparent strength when juxtaposed with an opposite or complementary hue (green with orange, red with blue, yellow with purple). Fiery autumn foliage appears more intense if set against a blue sky or when mixed with evergreens.

Intense, vibrant colors are more attractive than muted ones but they are not necessarily more desirable. The color theme of a photograph should support the main theme. A design which incorporates intense contrasting colors is visually exciting and the eye bounces back and forth between the competing hues. A contrasting color scheme suits dynamic picture themes that express action, conflict, joy, anger, or celebration; it is not suitable for portraying passive, introspective themes. Contrasting color schemes are volatile and can become confusing. Direct, simple designs usually are the most effective.

Harmonious color schemes are those composed of one or two similar hues, such as blue, turquoise, and green, but they may be made up of contrasting colors like red and blue if an intermediate hue (purple) is incorporated to create a smooth link between the two

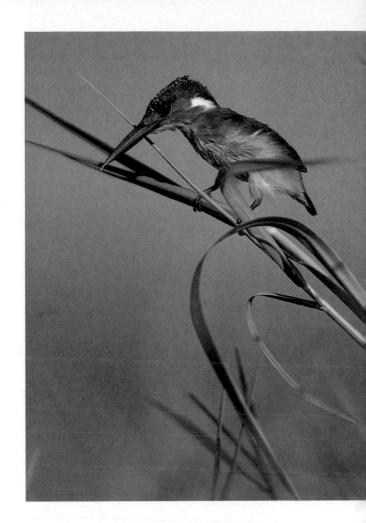

*MALACHITE KINGFISHER PERCHED ON A GRASS STEM: The vivid plumage of this tiny bird results from the juxtaposition of complementary colors — red and blue, green and orange. It is further enhanced by strong frontlighting from the sun. Preoccupied with fishing, the kingfisher did not notice my approach in a floating blind.*

*TEXAS BLUEBONNETS AND PAINTBRUSH: The hazy conditions of this scene reduced contrast so that the pure hues of these wildflowers appeared almost pastel. The combination of the complementary reds and blues, however, restores strength to the colors, and a compelling pattern results. When I came upon this expanse of wildflowers in the Texas hill country, there seemed little to do but frame up the most intense concentration of blooms and begin shooting. I used a 300 mm lens set at f/11 and a one second exposure. Although a smaller aperture was preferable for more depth of field, intermittent breezes disturbed the flowers, preventing the longer shutter speed this would have required. Even so, I had to time the shutter release to catch the scene between breezes.*

**ELEPHANTS ON THE MORNING SAVANNAH:** *During twilight certain wave lengths of light are filtered out by atmospheric haze, dust, or pollutants, thus reducing the range of the color spectrum and producing a harmonious color scheme. The warm hues that dominate this scene complement the peaceful theme of the composition.*

primary colors. A picture built with color harmony produces a coherent visual effect. Color harmony suits images with calm, peaceful themes and those incorporating horizontal lines and smooth shapes.

The effect of color on the image is pervasive. It helps to distinguish and identify the subjects of the composition, it communicates mood and emotion, and in many pictures its sensory appeal is strong enough that it alone acts as the central theme. Color is an integral part of our perceptive process, our dreams, our memories, and our personality. It will work best in your photographs if you approach it intuitively, using it in a way that simply feels right. This changes with each day and each year, and an openness to new color experiences keeps you in touch with your color instincts.

### The Visual Center of Interest

Most photographs have a visual center of interest, that is, one picture element that dominates the composition. In its most simple application, it is a picture of something — a cheetah, a maple leaf, a canyon. The center of interest orchestrates the design. It determines the nature and arrangement of all the other elements of the composition.

In nature photography the composition process is primarily one of elimination. You frame and focus on the center of interest and then examine the rest of the scene for elements that may detract from it. This includes anything that is brighter or of a more interesting

*OSPREY AT SUNSET: The sun is the most attractive element in this composition and the basis for the arrangement of the other picture components. The eye returns repeatedly to the sun during its exploration of the various parts of the picture. This image is what I call a 'club sandwich'; it is a composite of three different slides: the sunset scenic, the silhouette of the osprey with the fish, and the distant flock of ibises. All three transparencies were made on the same night along the Myakka River in southern Florida.*

shape. These elements can be eliminated or subdued in a variety of ways, such as changing the camera angle or moving in closer to the subject. Less often you may incorporate new elements in the scene that reinforce or support the center of interest. In the case of a portrait of a speeding roadrunner, it might be a cactus (to show habitat) or a streaked background (to show movement).

Where to locate the center of interest within the frame can only be determined in the context of the other design factors. The prime real-estate of any picture is the center. More than any other spot this is where the eye is most likely to begin its exploration. If you place the center of interest in this position it creates a static design — an effect that is rarely desirable. The eye settles on the center of interest immediately, scrutinizes it periodically, and then scans the remainder of the frame for anything else of interest. As it has already found your most compelling element, it soon returns for another look, grows bored, and asks you to turn the page or move along to the next exhibit.

Suppose you leave the most valuable area of the frame empty and place the center of interest elsewhere. The eye enters in the middle, finds nothing of interest, and begins to scan the frame. Sooner or later it finds the main subject but on the way it has come across other elements of interest. Now it is having fun. When all is seen, the eye gravitates back

to the center of the frame, but again it finds nothing and begins the search anew, perhaps this time taking a different path to the main subject. The dynamism of this process excites our visual sense and sustains interest in the photo.

The visual power of the main subject determines how far from the center it can be placed. If there are other equally powerful visual elements, then it can become dominant only by occupying the central area of the frame. A main subject that has strong visual properties can be placed almost anywhere and it will be discovered by the eye. If it is kept too near one edge and the remainder of the composition has little to sustain visual interest, the eye quickly becomes aware of this empty

**MOUSE-HUNTING COYOTE:** *The most interesting element in this photograph, the pouncing coyote, was kept away from the center of the frame to avoid a static design. Space was left in front of the animal to absorb its visual momentum. Due to the neutral character of the other picture elements, the coyote would be recognized as the center of interest even if it were positioned at the edge of the frame. Its conventional placement about one third of the way into the frame indicates that this is a simple portrait rather than a presentation of a more complex concept. Thanks to my ridgetop position and a favorable wind, I was able to photograph the coyote unnoticed for about 15 minutes. The grassy slope was tilted toward the camera so that the depth of field, though limited by the use of a 500 mm lens at maximum aperture, encompassed most of the hillside.*

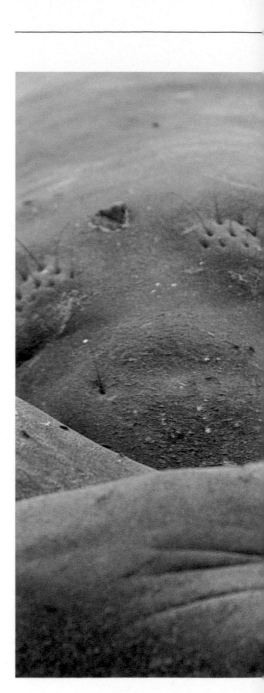

region and avoids it on subsequent travels. When this happens the picture is said to be unbalanced and confusion or boredom results.

### The Central Theme

Another basic composition strategy is to structure the design about a central theme. These kinds of photographs express an idea, relationship, or concept using a number of equally attractive picture elements. Suppose the idea is to express the abundance of African plains animals — a picture of hundreds of

**ROARING ELEPHANT SEAL:** *Unlike the photograph opposite, this composition is based on a visual center of interest — the seal's open mouth, which dominates through its strong color and emotional attraction as subject matter.*

wildebeest spreading beyond the photograph's borders. No single animal appears larger, or brighter, or sharper, or different. If an individual element did exhibit visual priority, the viewer would give too much attention to it and the idea of abundance, expressed co-operatively by the mass of animals, would be lost. The success of a theme such as 'winter tranquility' could be due to the combined effect of pastel colors, soft shapes, and a horizontal flow of lines.

Some themes are purely visual, often finding expression as provocative patterns or colors, or a dynamic arrangement of similar figures — a cluster of blue mounds or a splash of red and green. A photograph of strictly visual appeal is pure in its artistic intent and is as valid as those photographs with literal

meaning. One of the ways photography achieves its uniqueness is through communicating ideas and feelings difficult or impossible to express in words.

It often happens that a photograph whose message is primarily thematic also has a visual center of interest. It may be a grove of trees in a landscape picture or a single pair of piercing eyes in a wolf pack's portrait. Such photos can be unusually compelling, for the idea they present is not only provocative but it is also strongly organized about a single visual element.

## Rhythm

An integral component of all natural processes — the cadence of a running antelope, the rise and fall of snowshoe hare populations, the geometric swirl of the cosmos, the pattern of a sneeze — rhythm is a familiar and comforting part of our reality. It is used often as a basic principle of design, generating simple visual delight.

Visual rhythm arises from a repetition of accent and interval. On a simple level it is a single, uniform accent at regular intervals

*SLEEPING ELEPHANT SEALS: This composition is structured about a central theme. A number of picture elements — the soft gray and brown tones, the curved intersecting lines, and the rounded shapes — work together to present an abstracted treatment of sleeping elephant seals. The identity of the subjects is not immediately evident to the viewer, but once he recognizes the elephant seals, he can appreciate the ironic manner in which they are treated.*

which can be seen, for example, in a picket fence. More interesting rhythms incorporate repetitions of varied sequences or unit parts of greater complexity. Burrowing owlets, lined up smallest to largest, is a more complex rhythm that also suggests movement. Visual rhythms occur everywhere in infinite variety.

Many rhythms encountered in the field need further refining. If there is a discordant element that interrupts and weakens the pattern, you try to eliminate it. Often this can be done by a change in camera angle or magnification. With moving subjects — a string of ducklings, for example — the shot can be timed to catch the group when the pattern is most uniform. Sometimes, you may wish to take the opposite approach, especially when the pattern becomes monotonous, and include a break in the rhythm. This can create unexpected irony and add a further dimension to the theme.

*IMPALA HERD ON THE ALERT: Timing and camera angle were important in achieving this rhythmic arrangement of graphic elements. The impala were nervous and would stop feeding occasionally and bunch up for security, momentarily creating this strong pattern of legs, bodies, and heads. For this picture, the camera angle was at right angles to the elongated shape of the herd, allowing most of the animals to be included in the depth of field zone. Approaching the impala in a small jeep which acted as a blind, I made the picture about 30 minutes after sunrise using a 500 mm lens, warming filter, and Fujichrome 50.*

### Controlling the Elements

There are many photographic methods you can use to organize the elements of the scene into an effective composition. Your approach to any specific method should be based on how the principle of visual dominance affects the intended theme. Photography requires you to make many decisions. Here are some of the crucial ones.

* Choosing an appropriate subject, one that expresses your purpose most forcefully.

* Adjusting the camera position for the best angle on the subject.

* Selecting the camera-to-subject distance.

* Timing the moment of exposure to capture the scene or subject when it best expresses your purpose.

* Using the most appropriate film and filtration.

* Selecting an appropriate focal length.

* Planning the shooting session for the best light.

* Adjusting the camera position for the appropriate angle of light.

* Selecting the degree of exposure.

* Choosing an aperture that produces the necessary depth of field.

* Choosing a shutter speed that controls motion.

The last two techniques are special camera handling procedures that are discussed below.

### APERTURE AND DEPTH OF FIELD

The size of the lens opening, or aperture,

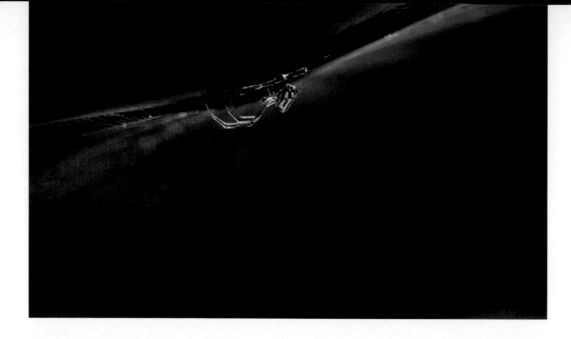

**SPIDER IN WEB:** *High magnification resulted in a depth of field that encompasses only the spider and a narrow band of the web. The contrasting soft focus of the remainder of the scene gives added emphasis to the spider. The spider was further isolated by the camera angle, which placed it against a darkly shaded part of the forest. Even at a shutter speed of 1/2 second, the still atmosphere of early morning did not disturb the web, and I was able to achieve a sharp image using a 500 mm lens and bellows.*

**CAVENDISH BEACH, PRINCE EDWARD ISLAND:** *This photograph was made just after sunset with a 50 mm lens set at f/16 (the smallest aperture) to achieve maximum depth of field. By studying the scene with the camera's depth of field preview mechanism, I was able to adjust the focal distance so that both foreground and background elements fell within the depth of field zone. In the absence of direct sunlight, the sandstone's vibrant color becomes subdued under the diffused, cool light reflected from the blue sky. The subtle colors, varied texture, and contrasting scale of the beach rocks dominate the image's visual appeal.*

affects two aspects of the photograph. In conjunction with shutter speed, it controls exposure, as we saw in the last chapter. The size of the aperture also determines depth of field, that is, the extent of the photograph that is acceptably sharp. Depth of field extends further behind the point of focus (the sharpest area of the photograph) than in front of it, usually in the ratio of 2:1.

Depth of field can be judged accurately before exposure by activating the depth of field preview lever on the camera. Normally framing and focusing are done with the lens wide open to afford the brightest view. Just prior to exposure the aperture closes automatically to the chosen f stop. The depth of field preview lever allows you to manually stop down the lens. When this happens the scene becomes darker, but once your eyes adjust, depth of field can be evaluated precisely.

Depth of field is controlled by aperture size, but its extent is for the most part a product of subject magnification. Whether shooting a rabbit's whiskers or an alpine vista, how large to make the subject is one of the photographer's first and most important decisions. Subject magnification is determined by both the power of the lens (focal length) and the camera-to-subject distance (focal distance). Both factors are usually given priority over aperture size. Once magnification is established, depth of field can be set by choosing an appropriate aperture. The relationship is simple: the larger the aperture the smaller the depth of field.

Deciding on depth of field depends on the photograph's intended statement. Minimum depth of field can render the main subject in sharp focus but isolated within a field of soft, out-of-focus elements. This gives visual emphasis to the subject, which is usually desirable.

In just as many instances there will be elements in the scene, in addition to the center of interest, that should be rendered sharply due to their importance to the composition. This requires greater depth of field and is achieved by selecting a smaller aperture. The depth of field preview mechanism will allow you to judge the effect before exposure. Remember that any changes in aperture will require an adjustment in shutter speed in order to maintain correct exposure. With auto-exposure cameras this is done for you.

### Stretching the Depth of Field

Due to low lighting conditions or the necessity

for a brief shutter speed, both of which call for the use of large apertures, depth of field is often limited. It can be used to best advantage if care is taken to position the camera so that it is equidistant from important elements. A simple application would be to shoot a rhinoceros in profile rather than head-on. This camera position allows both the head and tail to fall within the depth of field zone even if it is of limited extent. If doing close-up work, you need to keep the film plane (camera back) equidistant from the centers of interest. In shooting a mosquito, for example, you would want the film plane to be parallel to the mosquito's body. If two buttercups were the subject, you would position the camera so that each blossom is equidistant from its respective section of the film.

Another method of maximizing depth of field, used most often in scenic photography, is to set the lens at its 'hyper-focal' distance. First decide on the shooting aperture. Next preview the depth of field and focus as close as possible without losing the sharpness of the most distant elements of the scene (often the horizon). The lens is then set at its hyper-focal distance. This also can be done mechanically by referring to the depth of field scale engraved on the lens, but the direct visual method is more accurate and convenient.

## SHUTTER SPEED AND MOTION

The duration of the exposure, or shutter speed, affects the photograph in two ways. In

*WESTERN GREBE STRETCHING: Although this picture was shot at maximum aperture, which resulted in minimum depth of field, the position of the camera, equidistant from the grebe's head and webbed toes, rendered both these important elements sharply. Wearing chest waders and carrying a portable blind, I was able to approach these birds loafing near their nest.*

conjunction with aperture, it is used to control the amount of light that reaches the film. Of artistic importance is its effect on motion, that of the subject, or the camera, or both simultaneously.

A photograph can interpret the excitement of motion in many ways. At one extreme, all action is frozen by the use of a brief shutter speed. At the other extreme, an extended shutter speed allows the motion of the subject to be registered as a streak or blur on the film surface.

### Frozen Motion

Whenever you are working with motion, it is necessary to consider the movement relative to the film surface during exposure, rather than what the subject is actually doing. Suppose that an adult hippopotamus is running toward the camera at top speed. If you were to peek into the viewfinder, you would notice that the animal, though moving quickly across the veldt, is but slowly growing larger in the viewfinder. A shutter speed of 1/125 second would be brief enough to arrest most of its movement.

On the other hand, you may choose to step aside and photograph the hippo as it rushes by. A viewfinder perspective would show the animal entering, sweeping across, and moving out of the frame in the flash of a second. A much faster shutter speed would be required to freeze the motion in this case.

Obviously the direction of travel of the subject relative to the camera is important in

selecting an action-stopping shutter speed. You should also be aware that different parts of the subject move at different speeds. In the case of the hippo, its legs would be moving faster than any other part of its body, so they would be the most blurred regardless of the shutter speed.

The amount of displacement of the subject on the film surface is determined not only by the subject's speed and direction of travel, but also by its magnification. The extent of blur increases as you increase focal length or decrease the camera-to-subject distance.

## Peak Action Shooting
There are several ways to increase the action-stopping property of a shutter speed. By

*NORTHERN GANNET LANDING: With its big webs spread and outstretched wings flapping, the heavy-bodied gannet's landing creates a commotion worth recording on film. This sharply rendered version was made at maximum aperture and a shutter speed of 1/750 second. It is the best of about 100 exposures made in the hope of capturing such behavior. Most of the pictures were out of focus or caught the bird with its wings in an unappealing position. The blurred version was not as difficult to make. I used a shutter speed of 1/30 second and a small aperture (f/16), which produced more depth of field and made focusing errors less apparent.*

timing the exposure, you can capture the subject at a peak or break in the action. A bird is almost motionless, but still airborne, just prior to landing. Its wing beats are stationary for a millisecond at the beginning and end of each stroke. The rise and fall of a bounding impala offers the opportunity for freezing motion at the apex of each leap. These situations usually transpire too rapidly for the photographer accurately to time the moment to release the shutter. Luck and persistence play a part and a rapid motor drive enhances your chances.

## Panning

Another way to reduce blurring is to pan with the subject. This works best if you keep the camera moving smoothly both before and after the exposure. The tendency is to stop panning as you release the shutter, which can disturb the synchrony of the procedure at the most critical moment. Panning helps reduce blur in the main subject, but stationary elements within the scene will become streaked due to the camera movement. This usually infuses the picture with a strong impression of motion.

**ZEBRA HERD ON THE MOVE:** These zebras were not running as fast as they appear to be in the photograph — in fact they were walking. By using a shutter speed of 1/4 second and panning as the animals passed, the background became streaked, creating an impression of speed. The slow shutter speed causes fast-moving parts of the animals, the legs, for example, to blur more than others. The effect is made dramatic by the zebras' unique coloration.

Intentionally choosing a shutter speed that produces noticeable blur in a moving subject is exciting but somewhat unpredictable. It is most commonly used when photographing streams to enhance the sensuous movement of the water. In order not to confuse the viewer, the blurring effect should appear obvious. This usually calls for a shutter speed of 1/15 second or longer. The camera is tripod-mounted so that any stationary picture elements remain sharp, accentuating by contrast the water's movement. A watercourse with froth and bubbles produces the most pleasing results.

The intentional blurring of moving elements in the composition creates a powerful visual impact, perhaps because this sensation is unavailable to the naked eye except through photography. In addition to water, you can try the blurring technique on any moving subject — falling snow, a speeding hummingbird, stars in the night sky. The key considerations are exposure duration and relative speed of the various moving components — camera, main subject, and secondary subjects. Exploring motion with a still camera is a fascinating endeavor with unlimited possibilities and many surprises.

# Chapter Four

# Nature Up Close

An icy January morning and a chickadee perches immobile on a naked branch, a lonely puff of feathers fluffed against the cold. Clouds of condensing water vapor jetting rhythmically from each tiny nostril are trans-illuminated by the pale winter sun. A tiny scene waiting to be discovered by the photographer. Capturing such intimate views requires the use of special close-up techniques. The specific approach depends on the degree of magnification of the subject.

### SPECIAL EQUIPMENT
In close-up photography subject magnification is measured with reference to the size of a single frame of film. If the subject has the same real life dimensions as it does on film, it is said to be recorded life-size (or 1x life-size). A frame-filling portrait of a grasshopper on 35 mm film would be approximately life-size because a grasshopper is about as long as a frame of 35 mm film — likewise for a giraffe's nostril. A frame-filling portrait of a house fly would be about 4x life-size, and the same type of shot of a chipmunk would be about 1/5 life-size.

Standard lenses generally focus only close enough to render a tight portrait of a human head (about 1/8 to 1/10 life-size). Close-up photography calls for the use of close-focusing lenses or accessories that extend the focusing range of standard lenses.

**HONEYBEE ON WILD COLUMBINE:** *Reproduction ratios in close-up photography compare the actual size of the subject with its size as recorded on film. Shown above is the film section on which this honeybee was photographed. From this plate it can be discerned that the insect was recorded at about 1/2 life-size. The honeybee was photographed under natural sunlight with a 200 mm lens and bellows. I pre-framed an attractive blossom and waited for a bee to arrive. To lower lighting contrast I laid a reflector on the ground beneath the flower, which bounced light into the shaded areas. Bees poke a hole in the swollen end of the long spurs of columbine to get at the nectar.*

**PAINTBRUSH AND PINE CONES:** *This study of Indian paintbrush and ponderosa pine cones in Yosemite National Park was made with a 50 mm macro lens. The camera was angled straight down at the forest floor, which resulted in an unusual treatment of perspective, one similar to that seen in aerial photographs. For this technique it is necessary to use a tripod with legs that spread wide enough to be positioned outside the picture area. Because all of the subject elements rested on a single plane (the forest floor), only shallow depth of field was needed to achieve sharpness throughout the scene. I shot at f/5.6 and 1/30 second using both a polarizing and a warming filter.*

**INCENSE CEDAR BARK:** *An 80-200 mm zoom lens adjusted to its macro focusing setting was used for this photograph of a lichen-covered trunk. A macro-zoom lens is as easy to use as a standard lens. In this picture the curvature of the trunk required great depth of field to render all of the elements sharply. Most depth of field problems are solved with a tripod, which permits the use of the slow shutter speeds required when using small apertures.*

## Macro Lenses

The easiest way to do close-ups is to use lenses with macro or close-up capabilities. True macro lenses are expensive and produce high quality images, especially of flat surfaces. Available in focal lengths from 50 mm to 200 mm, most focus close enough to produce images 1/2 life-size. For greater magnification, lens extension devices are added. Macro lenses are also suitable for general work. Many zoom lenses have macro capabilities, although they generally do not produce as much magnification as true macro lenses.

## Supplementary Close-up Lenses

These simple lenses screw onto the front of a standard lens like a filter, and they cost about the same. With a supplementary lens attached, the focusing range of the standard lens is converted to a limited close-up range. Supplementary lenses vary in power from about +1 to +10 diopters. Usually they are sold in sets of three (+1, +2, and +3). These can be attached to the prime lens singly or in combination to achieve a variety of magnifications. For best results, attach the most powerful lens first.

Supplementary lenses have a fixed focal length that is the inverse of the diopter rating in meters. A +2 diopter supplementary lens focuses at 1/2 meter, a +3 at 1/3 meter. When the supplementary lens is attached to a prime lens focused at infinity, the focal distance is changed to that of the supplementary lens. You can work even closer to the subject by

adjusting the focusing ring on the prime lens to a nearer distance. The focal distance of a supplementary lens remains the same regardless of the prime lens in use. As a result, magnification increases as the focal length of the prime lens increases.

The best way to judge the degree of magnification is to attach the supplementary lens to the camera and study the scene through the viewfinder. With a little experience, it is easy to choose the appropriate combination of prime and supplementary lenses.

Supplementary lenses have a number of advantages besides low cost. They are small and attach quickly to the lens. Unlike extension tubes and bellows, they do not reduce light transmission to the film. Image quality is satisfactory up to about 1/3 life size — suitable for tight shots of subjects such as frogs, butterflies, and large wildflowers. The easiest and least expensive way to get a feeling for close-up photography is to start with a single +3 diopter supplementary lens. If you enjoy the results, then extension tubes and bellows provide the best means of further exploring the close-up world.

**GOOSE-NECKED BARNACLES:** *The intertidal zones of most beaches offer good opportunities for close-up photographs. You will find many small animals with unusual colors and shapes. Some of them — barnacles, sea urchins, mussels — live in colonies, which can be photographed to create strong patterns. For best results, work when the tide is low and the skies are overcast. Goose-necked barnacles are found in the lower region of the tidal zone, usually on the walls of rock ledges facing the sea. A narrow chasm separated me from this group, but I was able to record a close-up view by using a 300 mm lens with an extension tube.*

**BULL KELP AT LOW TIDE:** *Only when I examined this bedraggled pile of kelp at close range did I appreciate the rich texture and shifting color. The slick, undulating surface of the kelp strongly reflected light from the cloud cover above, changing its appearance each time the camera position was shifted. The composition is organized around the yellow edges of the individual kelp blades, framing them so that they move diagonally through the design. The vertical position of the camera was adjusted for maximum reflection from the surface of the blades. Reflections can be controlled in the intertidal zone with a polarizing filter and, on overcast days, by shielding the subject from cloud reflections with a black umbrella.*

94

### Extension Tubes and Bellows

If you focus a lens from infinity to its closest focusing distance you will notice that the lens elements move further from the body of the camera. Extension tubes and bellows continue this process, allowing the lens to focus even closer and providing even more magnification. Lens extension devices can be used with any lens that fits the camera, and being nothing more than hollow light-tight cylinders, they do not affect the quality of the prime lens.

Extension tubes are made in various lengths and can be purchased separately or in sets, usually of 10 mm, 15 mm, and 25 mm lengths. Automatic extension tubes are designed to permit full use of the camera's operational features. They are worth the extra cost over semi-automatic or manual tubes, which are not as convenient for shooting moving subjects.

Extension bellows operate on the same principle as extension tubes. They are composed of two metal plates, one adapted to fit on the camera and the other to the lens. These plates are joined by a light-proof leather bellows and slide along a pair of rails that keeps the whole assembly stable. The bellows is continuously adjustable and most types extend from about 50 mm to 200 mm. When making TTL exposure readings with a bellows, it is necessary to stop the lens down to shooting aperture. Some models can be fitted with a double cable release, which allows brighter focusing and more rapid shooting once the exposure has been set.

Bellows are especially suited for working at life-size magnifications and greater. The ideal type has a built-in focusing rail, which allows the camera-bellows-lens assembly to be moved smoothly and with great precision toward the subject, avoiding the awkward necessity of moving the tripod. A focusing rail can be added separately. If you are doing a lot of high magnification work, it can be attached at right angles to the built-in focusing rail to make fine adjustments to the camera's lateral position.

### Using Lens Extenders

In practice I decide what combination of lens and lens extension to use by putting them on the camera and viewing the subject. With a little experience, you soon get to know what a given combination will do — the amount of magnification that results and the distance from the subject you must work. If your intended subject happens to be wild and still at large (a butterfly or bird), simply set up on a reasonable facsimile and begin your actual approach when all the needed adjustments are complete.

If you wish to determine subject magnification in a more deliberate manner, use this equation: *Magnification = Lens Extension/ Lens Focal Length*. From this relationship, it is evident that short lenses have the greatest magnification potential. At reproductions greater than about 3x life-size, wide-angle lenses are commonly used. Camera-to-subject

*REFLECTING LIGHT INTO A FLOWER:* A small silver pocket reflector is used to bounce sunlight into the shadow areas of a wildflower.

*LONG-JAWED SPIDER ON CAMAS BUD:* Lying low to remain inconspicuous, this tiny predator keeps watch over its nearby web. When a victim becomes entangled, the spider moves in quickly to ensure capture. Soft natural light records the rich hues and intriguing depth of the scene, an effect that would have been difficult to achieve with electronic flash. The double track of the bellows moved the camera and 100 mm lens smoothly and unobtrusively into shooting position. In situations where precise framing must be maintained for numerous exposures, it is helpful to have automatic film advance, a feature that eliminates the possibility of the camera being jarred out of position during winding.

working distances can also be calculated but it is enough to know that telephoto lenses render the greatest camera-to-subject working distance should this be a critical factor.

### Reversing the Lens

When photographing subjects larger than life-size, standard lenses perform best if mounted on the tube or bellows in reverse position. All you need is an inexpensive lens reversing ring, which carries the added benefit of increasing the working distance while maintaining the same magnification. When using reversing rings the aperture must be operated manually.

A reversing ring also can be mounted between lens and camera without extension tubes or bellows. When used this way with zoom lenses, an extensive close-up focusing range results. The insignificant size of a reversing ring makes it an attractive close-up accessory for a zoom lens user with limits on the amount of equipment he can carry.

### Exposure Compensation

Extending a camera's lens for close-up photography reduces the amount of light that reaches the film. The standard TTL meter compensates for this automatically when working with natural light. If your camera also has TTL flash metering, exposure compensation again results automatically when used with a dedicated flash unit (one that links up to the in-camera flash meter).

With manual flash you will need to

**WOLF SPIDER:** *Photographed at 3x life-size, this spider's small size created a number of special problems. Due to the unwieldy nature of the close-up equipment needed, it was necessary to keep the subject relatively stationary during shooting. To calm down this fast-moving spider, I put it, stick and all, in the refrigerator for a few minutes while I set up the tripod and camera. When ready, I placed the now lethargic spider in front of the lens. To attain this high degree of magnification, I used a reverse-mounted 50 mm lens on a bellows extended 150 mm. Two electronic flash units provided enough light to shoot at f/16. The brief duration of the flash (1/1000 sec.) precluded blurring of the image due to camera shake or subject movement. The dark background results from the fall-off of light intensity from the flash. Usually objectionable, here it seems in harmony with the ghoulish nature of the subject and the overall dark tones of the composition.*

compensate for the light lost when using lens extensions. There are complex formulas that allow you to compute this amount precisely. In practice, however, there is no need for lengthy calculations. Accurate correction can be made for situations up to 2x life-size by simply increasing exposure by one f stop for each increment of extension that is one half of the prime lens focal length. If using a 50 mm lens, you need to open up one stop for every 25 mm of extension; for a 200 mm lens, it would be for every 100 mm of extension.

Another method of calculating the amount of exposure compensation necessary with your combination of lenses and lens extenders is to conduct some simple tests. Mount the camera on a tripod and meter an average subject — the carpet usually works well. Don't focus on the carpet but set the lens at infinity. Then add the lens extension and note the change in exposure for each different combination. Conduct the tests for the lenses that you frequently use for close-up work. Then record the data on a small card and keep it in your gadget bag for reference when using manual electronic flash.

## USING ELECTRONIC FLASH

Technically, electronic flash is the ideal illumination for doing close-up work. The brief flash duration (less than 1/1000 second) reduces problems of camera shake and subject movement and results in sharp, detailed pictures. The illumination is intense, and despite the loss of light caused by lens extension, small apertures can be used when great depth of field is required. It is easy to control both the intensity and angle that the light strikes the subject. By using appropriate diffusers, reflectors, or multiple flash units, high contrast can be avoided.

The problem with flash is that you are introducing an artificial element into a picture with a natural theme. The challenge is to make electronic flash look like daylight. Here are some suggestions.
* Sunlight, even at high noon, is diffused by the earth's atmosphere. To diffuse the light from electronic flash in a similar way, cover the reflector with a layer of white paper or cloth. If the flash is manual, you will have to increase exposure by one stop due to the decrease in light intensity.
* Position the flash away from the camera at an angle that could be taken by the sun. This might be beside or even behind the subject if opportunity permits. The flash (automatic dedicated units included) can be synchronized to the camera with remote cords. If the flash is positioned at an oblique "late afternoon" angle, use an amber-colored flash diffuser, or warming filter on the lens, to match the color of the light to its angle.
* Avoid the black backgrounds which result from rapid fall-off in electronic flash intensity. This can be accomplished by keeping the background close to the main subject, or by placing the flash equidistant from subject and background so that both receive a similar amount of light. You can use an additional

**HONEYBEE FEEDING ON A DANDELION:** *This picture was made in the field using a handheld camera and the flash system illustrated above. Once the angles of the flashes are adjusted and the magnification is set, all you need to do is move the camera/bellows/flash assembly toward the subject until it comes into focus. Exposure is based on the results of tests made with this system (as described in the text on page 102) or by using a camera with TTL flash metering.*

flash to light the background, but keep it as close as possible to the subject/main flash axis.
* Set up reflectors to simulate the trees, snow, sand, and other naturally occurring reflectors. With close-up subjects, such reflectors can be as small as the palm of your hand. Additional flashes can be used to open up shadow areas if the light is diffused and kept at least two stops less intense than the main flash.

### Close-up Flash Brackets

Indispensable for the close-up enthusiast is an automatic, dedicated flash whose light output is controlled by a TTL flash meter. Most major manufacturers offer this feature in their advanced camera models. Such a system solves all of the exposure problems associated with using close-up flash and lets the photographer concentrate on controlling the quality and direction of the light.

The best alternative to dedicated flash is to use the smallest manual flash unit available. High powered flash is not needed and standard automatic (non-dedicated) units are not programmed for close-up work. Inexpensive and about the size of a piece of pie, a manual flash can be attached to an adjustable bracket that positions it at the front of the lens. Various kinds of macro flash brackets are available. I like the one made by Lepp and Associates of Los Osos, California. This bracket and others have provision for using more than one flash. Brackets free the photographer's hands and keep the units in front of the lens where the flash will not be

shaded from the subject by the lens barrel.

You can calculate exposures using the standard formula for manual flash: *Aperture = Guide Number/Distance.* This is the basis for all the calculations on the exposure dial of the flash unit itself. The problem with these dials is that they don't provide data for subjects closer than a few feet. If photographing a small insect, the flash will be only a few inches away. Remember that the base exposure calculated in this way will still have to be corrected if lens extension devices are being used.

Usually it is simpler and more practical to determine exposure when using manual flash and lens extenders by shooting a test roll with the flash or flashes attached to the brackets. With a medium speed film (ISO 50 to 100), it is enough to make exposures at half stop intervals between f/22 and f/8. Use the aperture that turns out best as your basic

**GARTER SNAKE TASTING THE AIR:** *In the wild, snakes are timid, excitable, and distrustful of humans. This one was made docile by a stay in my refrigerator while I framed the camera on a tree branch in the back yard. Then I draped the snake over the branch, photographing it while it warmed up. In the photograph its tongue is tasting the air in an attempt to make sense of its predicament. A 100 mm lens and bellows were used with two electronic flash units. You can see the rectangular reflection of one flash in the snake's eye as well as the illuminating effect of the other on the undersurface of its head.*

manual flash/close-up exposure for magnifications greater than about 1/5 life-size. The relatively small f stop will result in near maximum depth of field. This is almost always desirable as the high degree of magnification makes it difficult to keep the subject in focus, especially an animate one.

If the subject is exceptionally bright, like a white butterfly, you should close down a stop from normal to retain the highlights. The reverse procedure is necessary for very dark subjects. Even though the amount of light that reaches the film is affected by the amount of lens extension, the aperture remains constant using the bracket system. Exposure does not vary significantly because the flash, being mounted to the front of the lens, illuminates the subject more intensely when it is brought closer, which results when the lens extension is increased.

### COLD-BLOODED CREATURES

The tiny frogs were all around me, yet I could not find even one. I turned off the flashlight and the night swallowed everything. I moved deeper into the swamp. The bottom, partially glazed with left-over winter ice, was hard and slippery in places, soft and sucking in others. Submerged deadfalls added to the confused footing. The air was saturated with the mating calls of spring peepers, tiny frogs I hoped to photograph. Hundreds of them, scattered about me, filled the black vacuum with a

*SINGING SPRING PEEPER: Not much bigger than a finger tip, a spring peeper is nevertheless a powerful singer. Its springtime chorus is usually heard at night. I used the handheld macro-flash bracket system described in the text for this portrait. In order to see the small amphibians in the dark, I attached a small flashlight to the underside of the bellows, angling its beam so that it intersected the plane of focus. This eliminated the need to make further adjustments while shooting.*

*WETLAND PHOTOGRAPHY: Marshes, lakes, streams, and swamps are the most prolific habitats for wildlife and plants. The best photographic opportunities arise if you are equipped to move right into the water after your subjects. Chest waders are indispensable for this, not to mention good balance and an insurance policy for your equipment.*

*AMERICAN ALLIGATOR: You can estimate the length of an alligator by multiplying the number of inches between its eyes by one foot. A small alligator is prey for many animals, and it was no surprise that this one was afraid of me. I had to be cautious and not approach too closely. A 500 mm lens and two extension tubes produced the high magnification desired and allowed me to shoot from a non-threatening distance.*

pulsing, high-pitched energy. Soon my ears were as useless as my eyes. I stumbled, gasping as icy, acidic water was gulped in by my chest waders.

My struggling silenced the peepers momentarily. I switched on the light to regain my bearings. Its weak, yellow beam played over the ragged cattails, groping for one of the frogs. Then a single, pure tone started up again and beside my boot, just above the water, squatting on a cattail stem was a tawny jewel, the size of my thumb. The frog concentrated. His throat bubbled out, showing a thin network of veins stretched over pale skin. Music filled the marsh. Excitedly, I prepared the camera.

Like the spring peeper, most of the wildlife subjects in close-up photography are cold-blooded. Mollusks, crustaceans, spiders, insects, fishes, amphibians, and reptiles represent the major classes of cold-blooded creatures that can be photographed without the aid of a microscope. They are generally easier to approach than birds and mammals, and being unable to regulate body temperature, their activity is more dependent on ambient temperature. A butterfly spreads its wings in the morning to collect the sun's energy; a rattlesnake lies in the shade during the middle of the desert day; turtles pile up on a pond log to sun bathe.

### Snakes

You would not attempt to photograph all reptiles with a 100 mm lens and an extension tube — not the crocodile that can weigh more

than a small car or the excitable cobra that rises up to look you in the eye on a jungle trail. But most are the appropriate size for close-up techniques. Few call for magnification greater than 1/2 life-size. Many species are wary of human approach and some are dangerous so that telephoto lenses are often necessary to allow a safe working distance.

The tactics for photographing most of them in the field are similar. First you must find a subject and to do this it is essential that you learn about the animal's natural history —its likely habitat, its preferred food, its reproductive cycle, its daily and seasonal routines. This also helps in understanding and anticipating the animal's behavior while you are photographing.

Snakes are challenging subjects. My first concern is not to get bitten. Some of them can inject lethal poison. This needn't deter you if precautions are taken: use a telephoto lens so you don't crowd the snake, work slowly and deliberately, monitor the animal's reaction carefully but with apparent casualness, and adapt your activities accordingly.

It isn't easy to get a snake to stand still long enough to take its picture. Another problem is the inherent shape of the reptile — long and thin isn't easy to work into an effective composition. Coiled up, the snake takes on more substance; a rhythm of color and texture is generated by the overlapping lengths of the snake's body. One technique that solves both

problems is worth trying, especially on sunny days when you come upon a snake in the open.

Without any cover to crawl beneath, the snake will head at full speed for the nearest refuge. Provide one for it and it will likely accept it with gratitude. If the snake is small, I place my hat over top of it. For larger specimens I use a jacket or shirt. A co-operative snake will take the cue, put on the brakes, and curl up under the garment. This gives you a chance to organize the close-up equipment needed to make the picture. I usually set up the tripod and mount a 200 mm or 300 mm lens with one or two extension tubes, depending on the amount of magnification I think is needed. Then, positioning the camera as near to the snake's level as possible, I frame and focus on the hat or shirt. When all is prepared except for last-second

*COILED WESTERN RATTLESNAKE: Seconds before this picture was taken, the snake was resting calmly beneath my shirt, which had been thrown in its path as it fled. It welcomed this unexpected opportunity to take cover and curled up. While the snake relaxed, I placed the camera directly on the ground to achieve an angle that would include blue sky in the background. When I lifted the shirt, the snake began tasting the atmosphere. The motor drive allowed me to make an exposure or two each time its tongue appeared. Although the photo was taken at midday, contrast is not excessive due to the reflective properties of the sand. After a few shots, the snake realized its vulnerability and moved off resolutely into the desert.*

fine focusing, I raise the curtain and begin shooting. You have to work fast because the snake soon realizes its vulnerability and heads for cover. You can repeat the procedure as often as it works but by the third time the snake likely will not take the bait.

Species that hunt in trees can be picked up and draped over a photogenic limb. The snake will not stay put for long so select the appropriate close-up equipment beforehand, set up the tripod, and position the camera for the best light, background, and foreground. Remember that the snake may have important business to attend. If it seems agitated or in a hurry, look for another specimen that has more time to spare. When you are done, carry the snake back to where you found it and see that it is comfortable.

Most of the snakes pictured in books are terrarium specimens photographed indoors under controlled conditions with the help of a herpetolgist or someone else experienced in handling reptiles. If this kind of work appeals to you, offer your photographic skills to an institution that houses specimen snakes. They will likely be willing to help you photograph their collection, especially if you provide them with slides or prints.

## Turtles and Lizards
A turtle should be one animal a nature photographer has little trouble approaching. For terrestrial species, this is true, but aquatic varieties are wary and quickly duck underwater when disturbed. Whether a turtle is wet

or dry, its shell shines. To achieve better color saturation, use a polarizing filter.

All turtles enjoy basking in the sun. At popular haul-out spots, pond turtles may pile up two or three high. Despite their sleepy impression, they remain alert and slip into the pond at the first sign of danger. Sandbars, logs, rocks, floating vegetation, river banks, musk-rat lodges, and stream shallows are likely basking areas. For these situations use the longest lens available. It may not be possible to creep closer without causing alarm. Instead take up a position near a well-used site early in the morning before the reptiles emerge. Get comfortable and keep still. It may take a while for the turtles to appear, but if you move slowly and quietly, you will have a chance to photograph them as they assemble.

If you come upon a turtle on land, detain it until you have a chance to round up a helper, and prepare the camera and tripod. Train the camera on a photogenic setting nearby and have your assistant hold the turtle in place until it stops squirming. Turtles can be stubborn about heading off as soon as their feet hit the ground, but they will soon co-operate if you are persistent and gentle in returning them to the ad hoc studio. Many of the turtles you find near a pond will be on their way to bury their eggs and when you pick them up they will loose a stream of water intended to keep the eggs moist. You might as well give the turtle a lift back to the water in this case, as it will need to refill before continuing with egg laying.

**EASTERN BOX TURTLE:** This turtle was photographed using the approach described in the text. First the animal was moved to a nearby clump of wildflowers, which were to be included in the design. My assistant held the turtle in position until I was ready to begin shooting. Taken just before sundown, the photograph exhibits the warm light typical of this time of day.

**CHUCKWALLA LIZARD:** Photography in desert habitats is made difficult by the stark lighting conditions resulting from clear skies. In this portrait the foliage helped to break up the sunlight, and light reflected from the rocks below lightened the shadows enough to show detail.

Some lizards can be approached fairly easily, especially the camouflaged ones, if you move in straight-on with little commotion. Don't let your body cast a shadow across the animal. It is best to use a long telephoto lens with extension tubes or bellows attached. Try to keep the equipment mounted on a tripod. If the terrain is rough use a monopod. Lizards like dry, sunny habitats and most of the time the light is bright but high in contrast, allowing the use of a relatively fast shutter speed. High contrast is reduced in rocky or sandy habitats where there is reflected fill light. If the subject is relaxed, you may be able to set up a reflector, or even more convenient, have an assistant hold the reflector in place while you concentrate on framing and focusing.

Some photographers capture lizards and take them indoors to a studio for photography. They build natural-looking sets and photograph with electronic flash. Some lizards may not mind this, provided they are taken home when the session is over, but most would rather not be taken out of their natural habitat. A butterfly net is used to bag fast-moving specimens. However, a word of caution about netting the fleet, carnivorous Komodo dragon lizard of Indonesia — some are ten feet long and weigh as much as a refrigerator.

## Frogs and Toads
Photographing these amphibians in their natural habitat is fun and yields excellent results. Marshes, swamps, and streams are the usual haunts of frogs and toads. Chest waders are ideal apparel for working in such environs. As most amphibians frequent the area near the shore, waders permit you to walk out into the pond and approach from deep water, in effect pinning them against the bank and blocking their escape. In addition the slope of the bottom places the animals uphill from your position and you can set up the tripod and work fairly comfortably eye to eye with the frog. Chest waders also let you crouch or sit down in shallow water while adjusting the camera or waiting for the frog or toad to start singing or to strike a better pose. Most individuals can be approached quite closely if you limit movement that is noisy, quick, or lateral. Singing frogs and toads are less apt to be deterred or distracted from their courting efforts when the weather is warm.

I like to use a tripod-mounted 300 mm lens with a bellows and work in natural light. Most

**BULLFROG:** *For photographing small animals in wetlands, my favorite system is a 300 mm lens with polarizing filter, double track bellows, and a camera with an auto winder and a remote electric shutter release. All of this equipment is mounted on a tripod and carried over my shoulder. When a subject such as this bullfrog is spotted, I set up the tripod, keeping the camera at water level. Then I move gradually closer, adjusting the tripod legs as I go, until I am in shooting position. In natural light finely detailed images are not possible without using the remote shutter release and tripod, because of the length of exposure and the power of the lens.*

**BLUE CAMAS AND HONEYBEE:** *Wildflower patches are ideal places to photograph insects. On a sunny day it is possible to make natural light pictures up to 1/2 life-size using fine-grained film (ISO 50 or lower). Shutter speeds up to 1/250 second are possible, depending on the maximum aperture of the lens. Even at these fast speeds, however, a tripod or monopod is recommended for sharpness. The limited depth of field inherent in close-up photography is apparent in this photograph. Only the pistils and stamens of the blossom are in sharp focus. After a few minutes of bee-watching, it becomes easy to predict when one is going to fly off, and exposures can be timed to catch this behavior.*

of the time my subjects are in the water, so even on sunny days there is light reflected up into the shadows. Nevertheless, I prefer overcast light for the greater color saturation and better rendition of detail. Even though you are using a tripod and electric release, exposure times should not be longer than 1/15 or 1/30 second for extreme close-ups, especially if the frog is floating, because its breathing will cause it to bob up and down.

For tiny frogs and toads, my close-up apparatus is the same as the one that I use to photograph insects (explained later in this chapter). Briefly it consists of a 50mm or 100 mm lens, bellows, and an electronic flash positioned up front on a macro-bracket. The short duration of the flash allows me the flexibility of handholding the camera. The black background which results from using flash is compatible with the nocturnal habits of many amphibians.

If I am working in a wetland after dark when the symphony of frog song is most intense, an auxiliary light is necessary to permit accurate focusing. To keep my hands free for adjusting the camera, I attach an ordinary flashlight under the bellows, angling the beam upward to intersect the view of the lens at the point of focus. The flashlight beam is wide enough to illuminate most of the focus range of the bellows/lens combination and it is unnecessary to adjust it further. You can still use the flashlight to find your way around the marsh.

## INSECTS AND SPIDERS

Any animal lover would be impressed with our planet's array of life forms, especially the little creatures that go unnoticed, too small for us to appreciate visually. There are over 250,000 species of beetles alone. Each individual of each species is single-mindedly preoccupied with tasks so crucial and familiar to us — eating the right foods, finding shelter and a compatible mate, producing and rearing offspring, achieving social acceptance and esteem. Close-up photography is your passport into this strange world of the six-legged, the poison fanged, and the probing antennae.

### Outdoors Under Natural Light

Photographing insects, spiders, and other small animals requires that all preparations — setting up the camera, adjusting exposure, framing, and focusing — be completed before the animal is introduced to the process. Once you have decided on a subject, the first step is to attach whatever lens and close-up accessory is needed to achieve the desired magnification. For animals the size of a thumb-tip or smaller, focusing adjustments are dispensed with once magnification is set. Instead you position the camera assembly itself the pre-focused distance from the subject. If working from a tripod you will need the aid of a focusing rail, or duo-track bellows.

Next, exposure is determined. I prefer to base settings on a TTL reading of a neutral gray card. For close-up work a gray card the

size of the palm of your hand is large enough. Be sure to angle the card so that it reflects a similar amount of sunlight as the subject. If working with film ISO 100 or less, the range of aperture and shutter speed will be limited. If there is little or no wind, a speed of 1/60 of a second is usually adequate to make sharp exposures if a remote release is used. Depending on the amount of lens extension, the complementary aperture will be around f/8 in full sunlight. It is usually calmest early or late in the day, or in a sheltered area — the lee of a rock outcrop or in dense vegetation.

## A Wildflower Stage

Any animal is difficult to photograph if its movements are quick and unpredictable. Framing and focusing problems are exacerbated at high magnification because of limited depth of field and framing tolerances. Staging the photograph reduces these difficulties.

A stage is any setting on which the camera

*BUTTERFLY FEEDING ON DAISY: When photographing insects, it is important that a subject's eyes be sharp and well lit. In addition to finding a cooperative specimen, this is one of the more challenging aspects of butterfly photography. This portrait was made using the staging techniques described opposite. A Flexfill reflector was propped up in front of the blossom to direct light onto the backlit subject. The angle was chosen to incorporate a shaded background. This photo was reproduced in favor of many similar ones, because of the dramatic way the light has illuminated the animal's proboscis.*

is trained and focused in anticipation of the arrival of the subject. The setting can be contrived (a winter feeding station), or natural (a bird nest or fox den). For insects and spiders, wildflowers are ideal stages. They are small, well-defined targets that permit accurate preparation of the camera. Insects are attracted to them to feed on nectar and pollen. In turn spiders occupy the territory to prey on the visiting insects. The blossoms are beautiful in their own right, but their smooth, graceful contours contrast effectively with the varied texture and angular shapes of spiders and insects. The petals often work as efficient reflectors to open up the shadow areas beneath the animals.

Insect activity at a flower patch depends on the maturity of the blossoms and their schedule of nectar production during the day. Usually the blooms are synchronized in this latter respect. The insects are familiar with the timetable, too. After studying the scene for a few minutes, I position the camera at flower height so that two or three blooms are within a similar range. These are my stages, selected not only for their beauty but for the attendant backgrounds and lighting. Kneeling or sitting on the ground behind the camera, I practice framing and focusing on these pre-selected stages. With this approach the picture opportunities are triple what they would be if you were targeted on just one flower. When an insect arrives, you are ready to start shooting a few seconds later.

**BUMBLEBEE HOVERING OVER ALPINE RAGWORT:** *Most photographs of flying insects are made using high speed strobe systems and automatic shutter release devices. But large, slow-moving insects like the bumblebee can be photographed with simple equipment under natural light, if you use staging techniques for advance focusing and framing. This bee was shot in bright sunlight on Fujichrome 50 with a bellows and 200 mm lens at 1/250 second and f/5.6.*

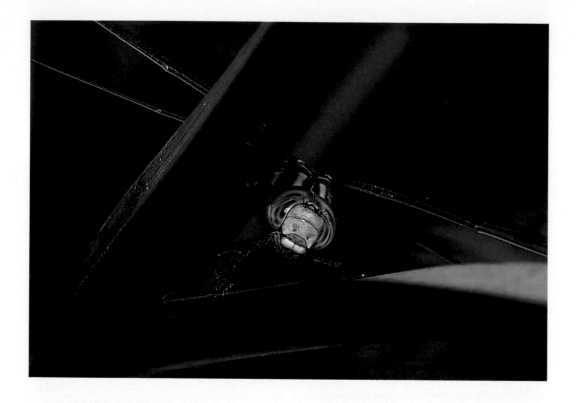

**GREEN DARNER DRAGONFLY:** *It is simple to make dramatic, handheld close-ups of insects using electronic flash. Brief flash duration eliminates the unwanted effects of subject and camera movement, and high flash intensity permits the use of small apertures for maximum depth of field. This dragonfly was shot using the insect instamatic technique described in the text.*

**CALIFORNIA POPPIES:** *For this wide-angle shot I placed the camera on the ground. The dynamic arrangement of blooms was the result of careful framing, and the color of the sky and the poppies was intensified by using a polarizing filter. A reflector bounced more light into the foreground foliage to prevent under-exposure and retain its fresh green color. Fujichrome 50 was used for its ability to reproduce clean greens.*

## An Insect Instamatic Camera

Shooting insects by natural light is limited to working with a tripod on sunny, windless days at magnifications no greater than about 1/2 life-size. The use of electronic flash makes it possible to handhold the camera at greater magnifications irrespective of ambient light conditions. The only practical way of using flash for close-up work in the field is with a macro-flash bracket as discussed previously.

Due to the unusual degree of magnification, the first problem is simply locating the subject in the viewfinder. Do this by positioning the camera apparatus at what you estimate to be the correct working distance and angle without looking through the viewfinder. This helps you avoid bumping any leaves or branches and frightening the subject. When everything looks about right, put your eye to the viewfinder and fine tune the image.

You will find this camera set-up awkward and heavy. A monopod relieves the weight and steadies the camera without limiting portability or flexibility of approach.

Insects perched on the end of a twig, tiny flower, or any pinnacle are the easiest to shoot. If surrounded by foliage, it is difficult to bring the camera into range without creating a commotion. When you spot a potential subject, the only thing to do is set the magnification. If it is a small insect I rack the bellows out; if it is large, I close them up — precision is not too important. You may need to adjust the angle of the flash units. Otherwise all you have to do is move carefully in on the subject and snap the picture when it comes into focus.

## WILDFLOWERS AND OTHER STILL LIFE

Elf cap, wild adder's tongue, maidenhair fern — romantic names for the fungi, wildflowers, and ferns that comprise the intimate detail of the landscape. The natural world is filled with still life subjects waiting for a composition. As picture elements they require the same attention to graphic principles as a Tibetan mountain range or sweep of savannah. Couple this with a creative, non-presumptive approach and your close-up macro photos will be enjoyed for more than just the intimacy of the view.

Most of this work will take place close to the ground and a tripod is needed to insure sharp pictures. The most convenient method of positioning the camera at this level is to use a Bogen (Manfrotto) clamp. It can be attached anywhere on the tripod leg and has a screw mount to accept a regular tripod head, the ball and socket type being best for close-up work. Forget about any other method. You may wish to use a right-angle finder which lets you compose and focus looking down on the camera. This can make photography more enjoyable if you are not physically flexible.

### Calming the Breezes

Sharp pictures are not possible when the wind, even a slight one, is moving the subject about. My advice is to shoot something else until it is

**LOW LEVEL SHOOTING:** The most convenient way to work close to, or at, ground level is with the Bogen clamp, a device that allows you to fasten a standard tripod head (a ball and socket head is best) to the tripod leg. This method provides plenty of working room behind the camera, and the only extra equipment you need to carry is the clamp.

**DAISIES IN THE WIND:** A number of special techniques were used for this picture. The low shooting angle placed the moving daisies against a contrasting background. A polarizing filter darkened the blue sky, and a neutral density filter reduced the brightness of the scene, permitting a shutter speed of two seconds (at f/22) to produce blurring in the swaying blossoms. A 20 mm lens enhances the feeling of freedom and expanse. During the exposure I blew on the daisies immediately in front of the lens to produce the motion.

calm. At high magnifications, however, when ambient light exposures are frequently a second long, this rarely happens.

In these situations it helps considerably to stabilize a botanical subject by anchoring a portion of the stem that lies outside the field of view. You can use a couple of rubber bands to fasten a stiff twig to the bellows or lens barrel, letting it project to the subject where it can be attached with a paper clip or small alligator clip. This can be very fidgety work if the subject is tiny. In practice, simply allowing the twig to lean against a strategic stem is enough to stabilize the subject.

Some photographers erect an entire tent about the subject. This not only becalms the set, but on sunny days it works beautifully to diffuse the light. On cloudy days it can result in exposures longer than necessary. Also there are the problems of the tent appearing in the background and finding a gadget bag large enough to hold it.

## Modifying the Existing Light

Overcast or hazy skies provide the soft, even light ideal for close-ups of still life, especially wildflowers. Even so, small, white matt or aluminum foil reflectors will improve color rendition and shadow detail. If the sun is unobscured reflectors are a must if highlights and shadow areas are to be registered simultaneously. For direct sunlight at midday, the easiest way to eliminate excessive contrast is to place a diffusing screen between the light and the subject. This can be a section of cheese

*INDIAN BLANKET WILDFLOWERS: High magnification and a large aperture produced the shallow depth of field evident in this photo. Out-of-focus blossoms can effectively emphasize other elements in wildflower compositions. When shooting under direct sunlight, shallow depth of field helps to lower contrast by softening the edges of shadows and highlights in the out-of-focus areas.*

cloth or similar material stretched over a frame. I use a white Flexfill reflector, which is good for reflecting or diffusion.

Another technique that is used to simplify or tone down the visual strength of the background is to cast a shadow over it. Use anything that works. (I usually use a friend's body.) Judge the effect in the viewfinder.

Experimentation with various lighting angles determines what is best suited to the subject. Translucent petals and leaves are suited to backlight, texture and shape are emphasized with sidelight, and frontlight produces good color saturation.

### Arrangements on the Forest Floor

Don't be reticent to adjust the natural components of your composition. You may feel like removing a distracting twig or adding some colorful berries to improve the design. Just keep in mind that for the photograph to be a convincing record of natural history, it must be believable. If you wish it to be a compelling piece of art, there are no rules.

**DOGWOOD LEAVES:** *Crisp autumn mornings are an opportune time to search the woods for close-up subjects. The warm hues of fallen leaves are often juxtaposed with the first, icy signs of winter. In this picture the subtle variations of leaf color and texture are effectively expressed due to the soft illumination, a result of holding a white, translucent screen above the subject to diffuse the direct sunlight. The photograph was made with an 80-200 mm macro zoom lens, warming filter, and Fujichrome 50.*

# Chapter Five

# Wildlife

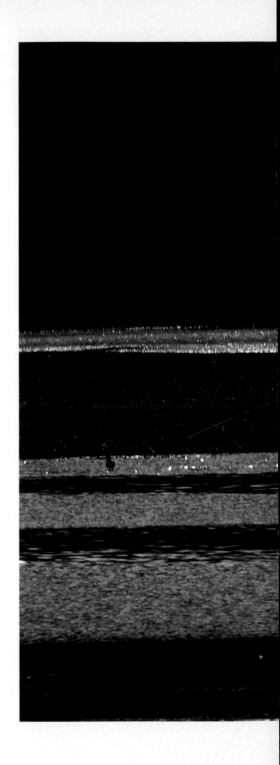

The wind began to whisper over the grouse's wings as the heavy bird descended with increasing speed. The whisper swelled to a roar, hurtled past my blind, and died abruptly as the grouse landed on the courting ground. It was quiet for a few minutes and then the surrounding hills erupted with birds. From all directions, grouse sailed down into the flats; missiles wrapped in feathers, fueled by hormones, trailing ribbons of energy that hung momentarily in the fading night. The ragged sounds criss-crossed and settled one atop the other. In a few minutes, my blind was surrounded by sage grouse, strutting, calling, and displaying their feathers. They were not aware of a human in their midst. Soon the sun rose and there was enough light to begin taking pictures.

To photograph a wary animal in intimate detail, it is necessary to get close and remain there. For this a blind is often indispensable. Most birds accept one with little suspicion, although reactions vary with the species and even the individual. They are less cautious during the breeding season, or when tired or hungry. Mammals, relying more on smell than eyesight to interpret their environment, are not as easily fooled.

### SIMPLE WAYS TO GET CLOSE
A blind is a box-shaped structure made of fabric stretched over a framework large

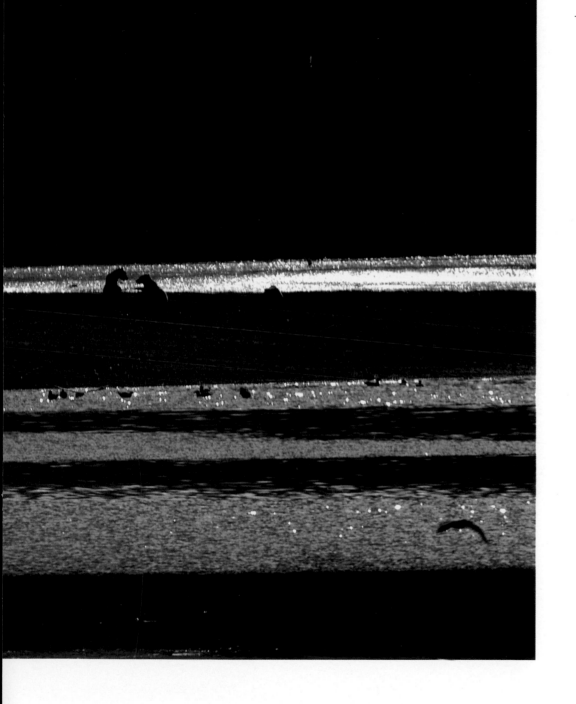

**WRESTLING GRIZZLIES:** *These young bears, grown fat on salmon, prepare for a tussle on a gravel bar in Alaska. I intentionally under-exposed the scene to retain the sparkling detail in the water and throw the bears into silhouette. The graphic quality of the landscape, strong backlighting, and the behavior of the animals were dramatic elements of this scene that coalesced only briefly near my campsite. The picture was recorded with a 500 mm lens at 1/60 second, f/4.5 on Kodachrome 64.*

**SQUARE BLIND:** A standard design for blinds, this one is made of cotton fabric stretched over a framework of plumbing tubing. When it is windy I use guy ropes to stabilize the structure. About 40 inches square, it is large enough to hide a tripod and a photographer seated on a small camp stool. Blinds that are simple and inexpensive are best suited to wildlife photography.

enough to conceal a seated photographer. Building one is easy and it allows you to customize it to your size, the habitat, anticipated use, and available materials.

* Use inexpensive materials so you can leave the blind unattended without worrying about theft.

* Make the blind portable. Use lightweight fabric such as rip-stop nylon. Flexible plastic plumbing tubing (1/2 inch diameter) works well for the frame.

* Don't hesitate to make new openings in the blind when necessary to attain the best camera position. A pair of scissors or a knife, and a tube of instant fabric mending glue are all you need to adapt the blind to unusual situations.

* Match the color and pattern of the fabric to the terrain. An inconspicuous blind made with camouflaged fabric attracts less attention from humans and is less likely to be disturbed.

## The Hoop Blind

Although not quite as easy to make as a conventional square blind, the hoop model has a number of advantages. Its circular shape is suited to windy conditions. The accordion structure adjusts to a range of heights, allowing you to shoot from standing, sitting, or even prone positions. It can be used in shallow water, such as marshes, lakes, tidal areas, or other wetlands rich in wildlife. The hoops float on the water's surface, permitting the height of the blind to adjust to changes in water depth that occur while stalking.

**TREE TOWER BLIND:** *To photograph birds, it is often necessary to erect a blind above the ground in a tree, tower, or a structure utilizing both, as is shown in this example, erected at a broad-winged hawk nest. Working in trees or towers is dangerous if you are not experienced, but it is the only way of obtaining revealing photographs of many species.*

**OSPREY FEEDING CATFISH TO YOUNG:** *I photographed this family of ospreys from a blind set atop two stories of construction scaffolding rented from a nearby supplier. Before erecting a blind, it is first necessary to consider its effect on the animals. Ospreys and many other kinds of wildlife are tolerant of blinds and the associated human activity. But some species are likely to abandon their nests or move to other dens if they are disturbed. It is best to work in small stages and regularly retire to monitor the animal's reaction to your intrusion from a non-threatening distance.*

**MAKING A HOOP BLIND:** *You will need 5-6 yards of fabric (54 inch width), contact cement, hoops or flexible plumbing tubing, and electrical tape.*

1) *Cut fabric into two equal pieces the same length as your height.*
2) *Glue or stitch pieces together long side to long side.*
3) *Sew four equally spaced 2 inch hems lengthwise.*
4) *Open hoops and insert into hems. Refasten hoops with tape.*
5) *Cut out and glue roof piece to wall section.*
6) *Cement open edges of fabric together to close walls. Leave top section open to accommodate camera.*

O'Donnell

The fabric for the hoop blind should be rip-stop, which is light and sheds water. If you can't find bona fide hula-hoops, they can be made from flexible plumbing tubing and short wooden dowels to join the ends. The only other materials needed are fabric glue and a sewing machine.

On land the blind can be suspended among poles (flexible 1/2 inch plumbing tubing works well) or hung by one line from a tree limb. The bottom can be staked or weighted with rocks. Similar methods can be used to erect the blind on a tree platform.

The most unique feature of the hoop blind is mobility. With the use of a shoulder harness, it can be suspended around the photographer and carried about while shooting. This is helpful in photographing animals whose movements are unpredictable. You can adjust your position for a better angle, different background or foreground, a change in magnification, or lighting angle. A monopod or a simple wooden bipod equipped with a ball and socket head can be used to support the camera. When possible, I shoot from a kneeling position, which reduces the size of the blind and improves camera steadiness.

## Using Natural Cover

The least conspicuous way of concealing your presence is to make use of structures that occur naturally and are an everyday part of an animal's life. In northern areas, blocks of snow can be made into a blind. You can simply

*COMMON MERGANSER: Kneeling on the marsh floor inside the hoop blind, I was able to photograph this fishing merganser without frightening it. Excited by the sight of prey, the bird swam very close to me on several occasions. Because the blind was suspended from a pole strapped to my back, I was able to adjust my shooting position when necessary. Birds are accustomed to deadfalls and other debris floating in the water and the sight of a moving blind usually doesn't disturb them.*

hide in the vegetation if it is thick enough, or use it to assemble a screen or even a full blind if necessary. Brush, log piles, trees, stones, bales of hay, and earthen excavations can be adapted to hide the photographer.

If the natural cover does not obscure you completely, wear camouflaged clothing, particularly on your hands, face, and any other part of your body that moves. I attach a small piece of camouflaged netting to the inside of my hat brim where it is ready to drop over my face when needed. It is transparent enough to see through for shooting. Your equipment, including tripod, can be disguised with camouflage tape or spray paint. All such camouflage products can be purchased in rod and gun shops.

### Shooting from the Car

Automobiles make good blinds, mostly because they can be moved to follow animals or to achieve a better angle. Generally, you are restricted to shooting along roadsides; never-

theless, many animals are found there because of the fast-growing vegetation. A 500 mm telephoto lens has produced the best results for me, especially if birds are the subject. A camera mount of some kind is needed to steady the camera. The simplest one is a beanbag pad jammed into a corner of the window. This works at shutter speeds of 1/125 second or faster. If possible I find a way to set up a tripod in the passenger seat. Bungee (elastic) cords can be used to anchor the tripod in place while the car is moving. Various commercial mounts are available but most are unsuitable for lenses longer than 300 mm.

The car should be turned off when shooting to prevent camera vibration. It is a good idea to stretch camouflaged netting, or any other fabric, across the windshield and side windows to hide you from the subject. Many animals will flee as soon as you brake the car, and it takes patience to find a co-operative subject in photogenic circumstances.

**SNOW BLIND:** *Pieces of snow were piled up to conceal the photographer from a herd of pronghorns. Even at a distance the blind did not fool the keen-sighted animals, but its strange presence aroused their curiosity and drew them near.*

**WAPITI COW AND CALF:** *Female wapiti are nervous about the safety of their young and approaching them on foot causes alarm. This pair was photographed from the front seat of my car with a tripod-mounted 500 mm lens.*

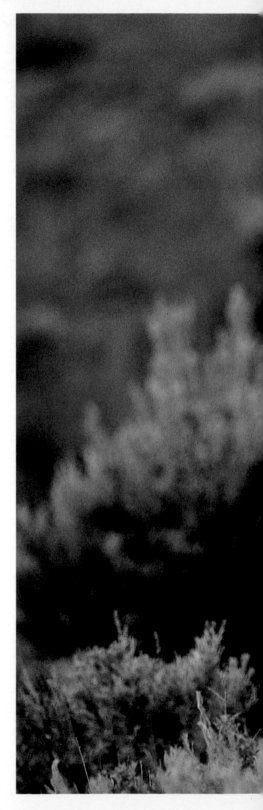

128

## BIRDS

Consider the aesthetic allure of the bird: the casual flight, the colored plumage, the supple form and delicate texture. A symbol for many ideas — peace, spirituality, freedom — birds are one of the nature photographer's favorite subjects.

Bird photography begins with an understanding of the animal itself. Most important, you need to be familiar with the bird's habits of feeding and reproduction. Each of the planet's thousands of species has a unique way of carrying out these activities. It's impossible to learn the details of each but an awareness of the general pattern is a passport into the bird's intimate world.

Consider a typical series of events that might lead to photographing a bird at its nest. Out for a hike in the spring you spot a bird with something in its talons. It is nesting season and chances are the bird is flying home. You head for the spot where the bird descended into the forest. As you get closer, a plaintive whistle breaks the silence — the alarm cry of a broad-winged hawk. The nest itself is built of sticks and decorated with fresh leaves, which is common for a bird of prey. No droppings are evident about the nest or trunk, indicating the young have not yet hatched. On climbing the tree you find two eggs, cream-colored with brown splotches. They are stained and dirty, clues that the eggs are close to hatching. The young will not be strong enough to risk photographing until they are at least a week old. You bide your time.

The first step in learning about a specific bird is identification, which is done with the help of binoculars and a field guide — a portable reference book that pictures each species in detailed color and identifies its distinguishing characteristics. Once you know the species of the bird, you can research information on its behavior. If you are planning to photograph at the nest, the main concern is to reduce the danger of abandonment caused by your activities. Through your study you also will gain insights into the daily activity of the species that could benefit photography in other ways.

### Birds at the Nest

A blind is necessary for photographing most birds at the nest. Although some birds are not deterred from their nesting duties by a human presence, most will not return until they are sure there is no danger.

The more experience you have observing and identifying birds, the easier it will be for you to find nest sites. This skill will be improved by studying written accounts and interpretations of field observations.

The location of a nest should be marked with a rock or stick to save searching time on subsequent visits. You should note the species and number of eggs or nestlings, quickly analyze the photographic potential of the site, and then leave. Your open presence at the nest should be kept to a minimum.

Only a fraction of the nests you find will be suitable for photography. These are some of

*REDDISH EGRET FISHING THE SHALLOWS: When feeding, the reddish egret lurches about the shallows in a drunken manner chasing fish. It is not fearful of humans and will approach closely if you remain still. A blind is usually unnecessary. The egret's fast, unpredictable movements while fishing make focusing difficult, unless, of course, you are using an auto-focus camera.*

*BLIND AT A HARRIS HAWK NEST: Most bird nests are found within 20 feet of the ground. Using two aluminum extension ladders and wooden braces, I can erect a tower blind at such nests in about 30 minutes. Guy ropes keep the ladders from toppling, a board for sitting is slipped across the rungs, and the hoop blind is dropped over the top. A wooden strut projects from beneath the seat to support the front leg of the tripod. The apparatus is inexpensive and portable. In this picture I am trying to judge the effect of lighting and camera angle on the nest before putting up the blind. One of the parent birds watches from its perch on a saguaro in the background. Working with towers is dangerous, and you should seek expert advice before attempting such photography.*

the important things to consider when evaluating a site.

* The ease of erecting a blind. This needs to be done quickly or in small time batches, and with little commotion.

* The lighting. Ideal lighting results if the blind can be set up south of the nest. This yields attractive sidelighting during the morning and evening. Shaded nests cause problems with color imbalance and inadequate light intensity.

* The background. I prefer backgrounds that are far enough from the subject to fall outside the depth of field zone; this emphasizes the main subject. A situation where the sky appears in the background creates problems with contrast and composition.

* The view of the nest. If the nest is not exposed, the vegetation should be such that it can be tied out of the way temporarily during shooting. Removing it endangers the young.

* The exposure of the blind. Other people should not be drawn to the nest area because of curiosity about the blind. It should be hidden or erected in a secluded region.

### Working at the Nest

When to start photography at the nest depends on the breeding cycle of the bird. The more time and energy the bird has invested in the nesting project, the less likely it will be to abandon the nest. Of course this tendency reverses itself as the young near flying age. This limits the effective period for photography to about one week after hatching to about one week before the nestlings leave. Photography at other times will likely be unsuccessful and harmful to the birds.

**ACROBATICS AT A GREAT EGRET'S NEST:** *In the lower part of this picture you can see young, down-covered egrets. They are not old enough to be left untended for any length of time, and the construction of a blind would have endangered them. Luckily, the nest was built on a low island in the middle of a marsh, and I was able to approach slowly in the hoop blind without disturbing the parents from their duties. I photographed them for about an hour and then slipped away. The nest site provides opportunities for exciting photographs aside from the expected shots of parents with young. It is ideal for making flight shots as the parents arrive and depart regularly. Feather display and other rituals of courtship take place at the nest, especially when the adults greet one another.*

The young of some birds, such as sandpipers, plovers, waterfowl, and others, leave the nest soon after hatching. For these species, the only opportunity for photography is during incubation. Fortunately, such birds are intent nesters and are rarely deterred by the sudden appearance of a blind. It is best to wait until late in the incubation period when the parents are least likely to leave and you have a chance to record the hatching process.

Setting up the blind should be done as expeditiously as possible, keeping in mind the comfort of the nestlings and reaction of the parents. The birds that seem to show the most alarm over your intrusion are usually the ones to calm down quickly. Do not keep the parents off the nest during rain, cold, or hot weather, and limit the disturbance to half an hour at a time. Position the tripod and camera at the best distance and angle, and then erect the blind around it. It is most convenient to leave the tripod set up in the blind. When you arrive for shooting, all you need to do is mount the camera.

Usually you do not have enough time to set up everything in one working session; this can be an advantage because the gradual erection of the blind may be less threatening than setting it up all at once. More important, especially for ground-nesting birds, is to leave intact the vegetation in the vicinity of the nest. A hint of a trail into the nest will attract predators — raccoons, skunks, weasels. Removing branches about the periphery of the nest will draw marauding crows, jays, and

other bird predators. Predation is the most common cause of nest failure.

### Inside the Blind

When the time arrives for actual photography, an assistant is needed to accompany you to the site. Once you are settled, the accomplice leaves, holding up a hanger bearing the shirt or jacket you were wearing and talking to it as if it were a real person. This ruse is needed to convince the parent birds watching nearby that all humans have left and it is safe to return.

Don't start taking pictures as soon as the bird alights on the edge of the nest. Give it a

*ROOFTOP STORKS: In parts of Europe it is considered good fortune to have white storks nesting on the roof. In small villages, roof platforms are erected to encourage the birds. I was lucky that the owner of this house near the Neuseidler See in Austria permitted me to climb onto his roof to record the storks' nesting behavior. I didn't use a blind but sat very still near the chimney while the young were fed and brooded. It was a Saturday evening and I was serenaded during the shooting session by music from a local beer hall.*

chance to calm down, either to brood or feed the young. Space the first few exposures to familiarize the bird with the harmlessness of the strange sound. Once the bird appears unfazed by the operation of the camera, you can shoot as fast as necessary.

### Birds in the Field

Away from the nest, bird photography is unpredictable. This can make it more exciting, for although there may be days when little happens, at other times a shooting excursion is full of surprises.

The first challenge is to find the subject. This usually entails finding the right habitat. Certain localities are rich in birdlife, wetlands and tidal areas being the most productive and easy to work. Explore such regions in your area to identify specific locations with good potential. Here birds can be stalked with a telephoto lens or photographed from a blind.

It is not easy to sneak up on a bird no matter how quiet or well-camouflaged you are. Getting close is more likely if you work with a blind, especially a mobile one. Cars and boats work well but they are limited by terrain and lack of maneuverability. Stalking with the hoop blind is often more productive. Here are a few pointers.

* Plan your approach before setting out, taking into account the lighting, nature of the terrain, and abundance of subjects.

* Don't set a course that will cut off the bird's

escape route. This may cause the bird anxiety and precipitate its departure.

* Concentrate on wetlands. Here you appear less threatening. Much of your body is underwater and the blind is folded up and floating on the surface.

* Be slow and deliberate in your movements. Stop if the animal shows suspicion. Continue when it relaxes.

* If often pays not to move at all for half an hour or longer. Birds will forget about you and some even begin to think you are part of the marsh, ignoring your subsequent approach.

### Feeding Areas

Hunger governs bird activity throughout most of the year. Becoming familiar with their feeding habits provides picture opportunities. In some instances, you have to work from a

**ROSEATE SPOONBILLS PREENING:** *Photographed about 15 minutes after sundown from a blind erected near a habitual evening roost, these birds were intent on straightening and cleaning their feathers. All of them stayed put during the 30 second exposure, and though their legs are sharply recorded, their energetic preening resulted in a blur. I set duck decoys around the blind so that the spoonbills would be calmed by the supposed presence of another species when they flew in. This trick can even be used with a floating blind by setting decoys on top, or attaching them to follow behind. As well as duck decoys, great blue heron and great egret decoys are effective in reducing the fear a blind may evoke in wildlife. All of these are sold at sporting goods stores.*

blind, in others birds may be accustomed to having people nearby and concealment is unnecessary. When working in the field you will find many such opportunities. Here are a few examples.

* Eagles, crows, ravens, gulls, herons, ibises, and others are attracted to fish-spawning areas.
* Vultures and other carrion feeders gather at carcasses.
* Songbirds feed on fruit trees and shrubs, particularly during fall and winter. Sometimes they become drunk on the rotting fruit and are less cautious than normal.
* Robins convene on wet lawns to hunt dew worms.
* Hummingbirds visit favorite flowers for nectar at regular intervals.
* Some birds, especially raptors and kingfishers, hunt habitually from favorite perches overlooking the gathering place of their prey.

*WHITE PELICANS IN FLIGHT: Each day on Kenya's Lake Nakuru, hundreds of white pelicans gather on the shoreline near the entrance of a fresh water stream. As the rest of the lake is alkaline, the pelicans come to drink and bathe in this small area, making it an ideal site for photography. An hour before sundown small flocks arrive and depart steadily. The weak light is unsuitable for stop-action photography, but it offers an ideal opportunity to make blurred motion pictures by panning along with the birds at 1/15 or 1/30 second. The pelicans' flight is slow and the pattern predictable as they glide low over the lake for great distances.*

You can usually enhance the photographic potential in such situations by taking a cue from the animal's natural behavior. Photographing hummingbirds is more a problem of accurately framing and focusing on the bird than getting close to them. I hang hummingbird feeders among their feeding flowers, hiding them from the view of the camera or disguising them with flowers. When the birds zoom in I know they will visit the feeders and I can have the camera prepared.

## Birds in Flight

The bird's mastery of flight has always stirred man's imagination. Photographing this phenomenon is one of the most challenging aspects of wildlife photography. First you must solve the problem of getting close to a wary subject. Then you must frame, focus, and build an effective composition from volatile picture elements. Should your skill and determination carry you over these hurdles, you must still be lucky. In most cases the action happens too fast to follow or to time the exposure consciously.

Photographing birds in flight requires prior knowledge of the parameters of the flight path. This helps you forecast the framing and focusing requirements, leaving only the timing of the exposure to your reflexes and chance. This can be done using a variety of staging techniques.

Suppose you are photographing gulls or waterfowl in a city park. First set the focusing

**AMERICAN WIDGEON TAKING OFF:** *Using the staging technique described opposite, I released the shutter as soon as I saw the duck thrust its wings toward the water. The slight delay in my reaction resulted in a picture that caught the bird just as it became airborne. For this photograph, taken under natural light at 1/500 second, the shutter speed was not fast enough to completely freeze the duck's explosive rise from the marsh.*

**GREAT WHITE HERON:** *While shooting brown pelicans, I noticed, some distance away, this heron take flight and head up the river channel toward me. Realizing it to be similar in size to the pelicans, I left the focus setting unchanged and followed the white shape in the viewfinder. As it approached the critical point of sharpness, I began shooting with the motor drive and made three or four exposures as it passed through the focal zone. A shutter speed of 1/250 second was enough to freeze most of the action, due to the head-on approach of the bird and its slow wing beats.*

distance to provide the desired magnification. Then follow the birds in the viewfinder until one flies through the pre-focused zone, in effect entering the set, whereupon you make the exposure. It's a simple technique that works well especially for birds flying across the field of view, as they remain within the pre-focused zone for longer periods.

Another more complex example of staging arises when photographing ducks shortly after take-off from the water. In this instance you not only pre-set the focal distance but frame an area of open space through which the duck will pass on take-off. This is your stage. But it must be positioned so that if you cue the moment of exposure to the duck's initial thrust against the water, the delay in your reaction will coincide with the duck's appearance within the frame.

In addition to attempting to set up a staging situation that permits you to eliminate as many variables as possible in advance of the brief opportunity for actual shooting, consider the following suggestions.

* Don't limit yourself to a shutter speed that stops all action. Experiment with the special effects that result from intentional blurring.

* When choosing a shutter speed, keep in mind that the larger the bird, the slower are its movements but not necessarily its flight speed.

* Much of a bird's motion can be stopped by panning along the flight path. When panning, squeeze off the shots gently, being sure to follow through after each one.

* When a well-defined image is desired, time

the exposure to catch the bird as it changes direction. Just prior to landing, the bird is almost motionless, with the wing and tail feathers splayed dramatically to break the momentum.

* The flight path is best anticipated just after take-off. In such a situation, you can finalize camera settings and framing relative to the standing bird.

* Study and compare the flight patterns of different species. Note the flight paths to popular roosting spots, nests, or other sites where birds gather.

* Keep the camera on a tripod with loosened controls. This produces smoother panning and reduces fatigue.

* Position yourself at right angles to the flight path to gain more focusing time.

* Remember that a bird, like an airplane, prefers to take off into the wind.

* A motor-driven camera and auto-focusing lenses will raise the percentage of good photos.

## MAMMALS

Unlike birds, which are noisy, colorful, and active during the day, mammals are silent, secretive, and generally nocturnal. Their behavior is less predictable and not often tied to a fixed location (the nest) as it is with birds. Wild mammals have highly developed senses of smell and hearing which alert them to the approach of a photographer before he comes within shooting range. Such characteristics create aesthetic, technical, and logistic problems. Solving them occupies much of the

process of mammal photography. Although not possessing the dramatic visual characteristics of birds or insects, mammals, being more closely related to us, are nature photography's most popular subject.

Many of the techniques described for photographing birds can be applied to shooting mammals. Develop strategies based on the animal's reproductive patterns and its need for food. As with other types of wildlife, one of the best assets will be a knowledge of the mammal's natural history. Study them in the field and in the library.

It is difficult to photograph mammals in areas where they are hunted or harassed by people. Most photographers specializing in

*HYENAS AT THEIR DEN: This hyena pack was photographed in the Mara Reserve of Kenya, where they are protected and easy to approach, if you are in a vehicle. They are nevertheless cautious, and the pups scurry underground if you make an unexpected move. I visited the den on several occasions at sunset, an active time for the pack as it readied for the evening hunt. During the day photography is less fruitful, because the hyenas are scattered through the grass or resting underground to escape the heat. I used a window-mounted 300 mm lens, Fujichrome 50, and a warming filter to enhance the glow of sunset.*

143

*MULE DEER IN ALPINE MEADOW: This deer was busy feeding in the lush growth, and although it carefully monitored my slow and labored approach up the mountainside with nose, eyes, and ears, it showed little alarm. It would have been more nervous had I come upon it from above, as a predator would. The telephoto lens resulted in shallow depth of field, rendering all of the scene, except the subject, in soft green tones. I spent some time photographing the deer's behavior, managing simultaneously to catch it with a mouth full of mountain lily and an inquisitive look.*

mammals work in national parks, in polar regions, or on remote islands where their subjects are tolerant of the close approach of humans. Even if photographing under such favorable circumstances, it is advantageous to adapt your methods to the animals' instinctive behavior patterns.

### The Nose

A mammal's sense of smell is something we cannot easily appreciate. To get an idea of its importance, imagine yourself wandering around the woods blindfolded. This is what a lot of mammals would feel like without their noses. In still conditions, scent spreads out from the source like pancake batter on a griddle, but usually it is carried to the animal on the wind. Even if you are in plain sight, it is wise to stay downwind of the subject. A steady crosswind will dispose of your scent, although a stray gust may carry it to the animal.

### Habits

Most mammals are nocturnal, resting in seclusion, perhaps in a thicket, a burrow, or high in a tree while we are busy working. Obviously you must co-ordinate your activities with those of the subject. Since photography at night, the period of greatest activity for mammals, requires artificial light and results in few satisfactory images, it is wise to spend your efforts at dawn and dusk, a compromise between good light and the availability of the subject.

As with birds, you can plan shooting

sessions to take advantage of the mammal's reproductive cycle. The rutting season is a good time for photographing hoofed mammals. The males are noisy and belligerent. Preoccupied with the fierce competition for mates, they are more easily approached than at any other time of the year.

Most other mammals bear their young in special sites — in a nest of grasses or in a burrow, hollow tree, or cave, beneath a windfall, or in a rock pile. Although the site may be in uninspiring surroundings and poorly lit, at least you can be sure of the presence of your subject.

Seals, sea lions, and walrus gather on established breeding sites by the hundreds or even thousands. Some species show no fear of man at all, others can be approached only cautiously and patiently. These species also have regular haul-out sites which offer good photographic opportunities during the non-breeding season.

## Stalking

When approaching mammals I normally carry a 500 mm lens mounted on a tripod and adopt an air of nonchalance. I may whistle, talk softly to the animals, scratch, or stare at the horizon for long moments as if preoccupied with something else. Sometimes I move closer by taking an oblique line of travel, as if my destination were elsewhere. If you are downwind of the subject a frontal approach sometimes works well, provided you keep your silhouette below the horizon. The main

**ANGRY GRIZZLIES:** *A female grizzly attacks a male that has just mauled her cub. The powerful male was unharmed and soon resumed fishing, but the cub probably died, as it was not seen with its mother the next day. This episode was photographed from a public viewing platform at Brooks Falls in Alaska. Here salmon congregate as they attempt to scale the falls on their way upstream to spawning beds. Scores of bears arrive during the salmon migration to fatten up on fish in preparation for winter hibernation.*

**SNOWSHOE HARE AMONG FIREWEED:** *Rainy weather in Denali National Park in Alaska kept me inside the tent for a few days, so I used the time to photograph some of the smaller animals around camp. A clump of fireweed transplanted to the front of my tent, and subsequently perfumed with peanut butter, attracted this hare into camera range and simultaneously provided a natural setting for the portrait. The overcast skies, forest shade, and active nature of the subject called for a fast film. I used Fujichrome 100 at 1/30 second and f/4.5.*

precautions when stalking are to stay low, approach from downwind, and keep your movements slow and deliberate.

### Peanut Butter Bait

My gadget bag always has a stock of peanut butter that I use for attracting and controlling the activities of mammal subjects. Peanut butter has a powerful, enticing odor, an inconspicuous color, great taste, and it will stick to anything. In addition, once attracted, the animal cannot carry it away, but must enjoy it in front of the lens. You can spread it wherever you would like the animal to pose. Sometimes you need to make a peanut butter trail to lead the animal into a photogenic set. It works best to use peanut butter in conjunction with a natural food source. When photographing squirrels, for instance, you can dab peanut butter on pine cones, wildflowers, and buds, and photograph them engaged in an apparently natural feeding activity.

# Chapter Six

# Landscape

The land does not flee the photographer's lens like a deer or jackal, nor spoil a picture with an untimely blink or yawn. Nevertheless, it presents great challenges. A painter designs his images freely. With a few brush strokes he can spread a slope with lupines or start a river flowing. Such control is not afforded the landscape photographer. His canvas is the planet itself, which each day is tempered by the changing moods of light and sky, shifting winds and weather, and passing seasons. Relying on technique, patience, and timing, he works in reaction to the environment, searching for a situation that can be creatively explored.

SHOOTING PROCEDURES

The landscape should be appraised for its potential for graphic expression. Does it offer provocative shapes or expressive colors? Is there a special interplay of line or unusual perspective? The changing character of sunlight influences such scenic qualities more than any other factor. An uninteresting view at midday may exude a compelling intensity at twilight, or explode with drama at dawn.

The appeal of a landscape flows from many elements acting together, but usually one or two dominate. It may be the color of a grove of trees, an expanse of sky, the sweep of perspective, a pattern of scattered boulders, or the rush of ocean

**SWEETGRASS HILLS, MONTANA:** This view southward across the Canadian border into Montana is framed by a telescoping arrangement of cottonwood trees. A carefully selected camera position made the most of this pictorial opportunity. I waited until sunset for the light to soften and evenly illuminate all parts of the scene.

**ROCKY MOUNTAINS NEAR MALIGNE LAKE, ALBERTA:** *As often happens in landscape photography, the choice of camera position for this picture was restricted, forcing me to use a long lens to achieve this composition. Design considerations aside, optimum clarity results when you get as close to a scene as possible to decrease the effects of atmospheric haze. To give emphasis to the cloud formations, I framed peaks of uniform size and shape so that no single one would become dominant in the composition. The black foreground and sunlit peaks work together to draw the eye into the distance, but just as forceful is the ominous effect generated by the darkness and sheer size of the cloudbanks.*

surf. Once the central theme is defined, you can begin to translate your idea into the language of film. You know, for example, that the color intensity of a grove of trees can be controlled by lighting, exposure, and filtration, that camera angle will determine the impact of the sky, that perspective is dependent on focal length, that the success of a pattern is a product of framing and magnification, and that shutter speed is critical in rendering the effect of moving surf. With experience the choice of photographic treatment for such diverse situations becomes routine, incorporated into a generally informal but systematic picture-making process.

Step I:

**Choose Camera Position and Focal Length**
Initially the camera is placed to achieve the most expressive angle on the key elements of the scene. Later it may be altered to incorporate supportive elements. The conventional position renders the scene with a typical foreground/middleground/background approach to perspective. Postcards nearly always portray the landscape using this method of organization. That it is used so frequently is evidence of its visual power. However, this approach can easily descend into cliché if the remaining picture elements are treated with similar convention.

The immediate effect of focal length is on the magnification of the scene, which may also be controlled by changing the camera-to-subject distance. As both methods are

**AUTUMN HILLSIDE, PENNSYLVANIA:** *The impressive feature of this landscape was not a great sweep of terrain, an intriguing arrangement of landforms, or a threatening storm; it was the color of the trees, and this is the feature I tried to emphasize. A 500 mm lens was used to frame the most intense patch of color on the hillside, which resulted in a flattened perspective and abstract tone. I shot at a shutter speed of one second to minimize camera vibration. To accentuate the dramatic colors, the scene was recorded on Fujichrome 50 film with a warming filter.*

interdependent, they are carried out simultaneously. If the shooting situation permits camera position to be adjusted for the desired magnification, perspective effects can be controlled by changing focal length.

### Step II: Framing and Focusing

If you wish to render the entire scene in sharp focus, the depth of field must stretch from the foreground elements to the horizon. Aided by the camera's depth of field preview mechanism, you can adjust the framing of the scene so that the view falls totally within the depth of field zone.

There is no technical difficulty in making photos with shallow depth of field. Low light levels are best suited to large apertures, which produce shallow depth of field. If there is too much light to open the diaphragm the desired amount, use a neutral density filter to reduce its intensity.

Framing the scene is carried out simultaneously with focusing and setting the depth of field. Once you have positioned the most important picture elements, check the periphery of the frame for distracting objects. An out-of-focus grass stem or twig may otherwise go unnoticed until the film is developed.

### Step III: Setting Filtration and Exposure

The final step is determining the exposure. First, however, decide if any filtration is necessary. The filter must be attached before light readings are made, as it will affect exposure. Usually lens aperture has been determined as a component of the depth of field requirements so that exposure is set by adjusting shutter speed. Sometimes the portrayal of motion takes priority over depth of field, fixing the shutter speed and relegating to aperture the task of controlling exposure.

Once you have determined the settings for a normal exposure, you may choose to adjust these parameters to bring emphasis to the picture's theme. Over-exposure dilutes the colors, reducing the definition and giving a lighter feeling to the image. For richer color, greater contrast, and a more serious mood, it is necessary to under-expose from the average reading.

A last check of the foregoing steps and you are ready to make the exposure. Unless you activate the shutter with the self-timer or a remote release, image resolution may suffer. If there are any aspects of the scene about which you are unsure, such as exposure, camera position, or focal length, now is the time to take some extra pictures.

### Timing

The moment that you choose to take the picture is as critical when shooting a landscape as it is when working at an osprey nest. When shooting wildlife, subject activity or position often provokes the exposure. When photographing the land, lighting is usually the critical factor. There is a time each day when the angle and color of sunlight illuminate the scene to best advantage. Weather conditions and time of year also affect the situation. Being in the right place at the right time is a product of planning, flexibility, and opportunism — all of which you can control.

### CONTROLLING PERSPECTIVE

A photograph is but a flat representation of the real world. There are inherent problems and intriguing insights that spring from both the process and the product of expressing perspective (the third dimension) on a two-dimensional surface like film.

The graphic factors that affect perspective are simple to understand and control. You can use them in a straight-forward manner to show distance and space in your photos or you can mix up the various techniques, expanding and compressing the scene all at once to play with the viewer's concept of reality and cause him to question his perceptions of the world.

* Close objects appear larger than identical ones farther away. You can express depth dramatically by including similar-sized elements (daisies, beach pebbles, zebras) in the same composition if you position the camera so that their size on film is different. The greater the size discrepancy the greater will be the impression of space. A wide-angle lens exaggerates the size discrepancies as rendered on film; a telephoto reduces them. To be most

effective, the size relationship between the perspective cues should be obvious. Rocks or trees vary greatly in size so that we don't readily process these landscape features as reliable clues of receding space. We know that poppies and caribou, on the other hand, fall within a fairly narrow size range and readily establish the scale of a scene.

The convergence of parallel lines as they recede in the distance (the banks of a river, railway tracks) demonstrates the effect of relative size cues on perspective. Size-dependent perspective is controlled in several ways: by the nature of the size cues, by focal length, and by camera position.

* Close objects are normally found lower in the scene than far ones. This is because our eyes are elevated from the ground. If you position the camera at eye level, the same expected perspective results; close objects fall at the bottom of the frame. A common

*POINT WOLFE RIVER, NEW BRUNSWICK: This picture demonstrates factors that create a strong impression of three dimensions. The distant rocks are overlapped by near ones; they are also smaller and higher in the frame. The banks of the river converge as they move away. Atmospheric haze makes far objects, such as the distant river bank, less distinct. These perspective cues are emphasized by the use of a wide-angle lens (20 mm), which increases the apparent space between objects. Although the camera was tipped downward, the distortion that resulted is not apparent, due to the inherent amorphous quality of these rocks.*

exception to this expected arrangement of perspective cues is when tree boughs appear about the sides and top of the frame. Like any exception it creates interest. You can use other cues aside from this cliché to upset the viewer's expectations.

* Close objects are found in front of far objects; they overlap. Trees, hills, or any landscape element that partially obscures another expresses depth. Adjusting camera angle to encompass or isolate an overlapping pattern creates the feeling of expanding space. A telephoto lens used in such a situation creates the opposite effect, compressing the space that overlapping extends.

* Close objects appear sharper than ones farther away. This is usually referred to as aerial perspective. What happens is there are more air molecules between you and far objects than near ones so that they appear less distinct. Obviously the greater the number of airborne particles, the greater will be the impression of space. Fog and dust in the atmosphere create this illusion of distance but without the corroboration of other associated cues of size, placement, or overlapping. This irony creates interest.

* Sidelighting reveals the contours and form of the land. It makes objects that may be important size cues easier to identify and compare. It accentuates the effect of overlapping by creating greater contrast between shadows and highlights to differentiate the receding planes of the scene.

**SEMIAHMOO BAY, BRITISH COLUMBIA:** *Although there are a number of three-dimensional perspective cues in this photograph, their effect is moderated by the use of a telephoto lens and the water-level camera angle. Both factors reduce the apparent distance between near and far objects. These spatial contradictions and the blurred surface of the ocean (the result of a 30 second exposure) work together to create a surreal effect.*

**DOUGLAS FIR GROVE, WASHINGTON:** *Few natural situations offer as much potential for exploring perspective as tree trunks and fog. The uniform diameter of the trunks makes them expressive size cues, and the fog dramatically accentuates aerial perspective. In the original slide, the trunks appear to be toppling out of both sides of the frame, the result of using a wide-angle lens tilted upward. In reproducing the photograph for this book, I re-oriented the cropping so that the left side of the frame was parallel to the trunks, creating an effect that is in some ways even stranger.*

## WEATHER'S CHANGING MOODS

Film does not record rain or snow effectively except under special conditions of light and camera position. A camera angle which places the precipitation against a dark background (storm clouds, evergreen trees, shaded mountainside) is ideal. Backlighting or sidelighting is needed to illuminate the rain drops or define the snowflakes, and it often casts helpful shadows across the background. Underexposing the scene may create more contrast and help emphasize the rain or snow.

The apparent size of the raindrops or snow flakes can be made larger by using a shutter speed 1/30 second or slower, which creates glistening vertical streaks or blurs. Double exposure can be used to turn a snow flurry into a blizzard. Make the first exposure of the entire scene and then refocus on some snow flakes that are falling closer to you and make the second exposure. Magnified in this way they overlay the first image. Under-expose each shot by one stop to achieve a normal exposure of the composite image.

## Lightning

Lightning usually doesn't last long enough to photograph by direct release of the shutter. However, if you set the exposure time for 20 or 30 seconds, it is not difficult to record its effect. Aim the camera at the portion of the sky where there is the most electrical activity. Open the shutter when you see the first bolt. You'll record only a portion if anything of this one. But usually within ten seconds another flash will occur. If you would like to record multiple flashes, cover the lens with your hat during the waiting intervals and you may be able to collect several flashes during the exposure.

## The Night Sky

A full moon casts only 1/400,000 as much light as the sun. This calls for exposures lasting from five to fifteen minutes using ISO 100 film at f/2.8. Faster film will of course reduce the exposure time. In any case the image that results has a dominant bluish cast and shadows are indistinct because the moon moves during the lengthy exposure.

Photographing the moon itself is much more within the capabilities of the film and camera. It is after all a subject that is lit by the sun and you can use the f/16 rule to set the exposure. A moon photographed with a normal 50 mm lens is not very imposing. Normally I like a moon as big as I can get it, so I use focal lengths of at least 300 mm. Shutter

**PIN CHERRY TREES ALONG THE RIDEAU RIVER, ONTARIO:** *Falling rain diffused the colors of this stand of cherry trees, an effect enhanced by the soft lighting conditions. The lack of color in the limbs and trunks focuses visual attention on the pastel splashes of red and green. These branches also link the clumps of leaves, resulting in a strongly unified design. When working in light rain I keep a small towel over the camera and lens for protection and to wipe my hands periodically. As soon as the opportunity permits, I dry my equipment under a hair blower, or, if I am driving, I set it over the heating vents of the car.*

speeds faster than one second should be used for telephoto shots to avoid the blur resulting from the moon's movement through the sky.

By using double exposure or sandwiching techniques, you can adjust the position of a poorly situated moon. First photograph the moon, framing it precisely where you wish it to be in the final composite shot. A focusing screen with etched grid lines is very helpful in this situation. For the second exposure you needn't rush. You can change lenses or move to a different location to attain the desired landscape elements. Keep in mind the position of the moon from the first exposure when adding the new elements. If shooting at dusk, situate a full moon in the opposite part of the sky to the sun if you are concerned about realism.

### The Sun

Although we normally think of the sun as a generator of light, it is a compelling subject in its own right. It is best photographed at dawn or dusk when its color and size are most dramatic. Cloud and atmospheric haze subdue its brilliance and create lower-than-normal contrast, allowing other features of the land-scape to be recorded simultaneously in the composition. On foggy days the sun will break through the clouds occasionally, but at only a fraction of its normal strength so that it can be incorporated in the scene without causing excessive flare or high contrast. The sun has

**SUNSET, LOWER MATECUMBE KEY, FLORIDA:** *The angle of the sun when setting or rising causes its rays to travel farther through the earth's atmosphere than at any other time of the day. Much of its energy is absorbed by the air, and it loses its customary brilliance. As in this picture, it can be included in many scenic photographs, especially of lakes or oceans, without producing lighting ratios much in excess of the exposure latitude of the film.*

**STORM OVER RED ROCK LAKE, MONTANA:** *The brooding intensity of a summer storm is accentuated by tilting a wide-angle lens upward to incorporate as many of the storm clouds as possible. This technique works best when clouds are directly overhead. A variable neutral density filter was placed over the lens to further darken the sky.*

such graphic strength that it plays a dominant role in most compositions regardless of the focal length used. The use of telephoto lenses increases its dramatic impact.

Exposures ranging over three or four f stops may be suitable for a sunset/sunrise scene. With the great range of contrast, something is bound to be properly exposed. The most dependable approach is to make a spot reading of a portion of the sky with strong saturated color, thereby insuring an accurate rendition of what is usually an important part of the scene. Take care not to let the direct rays of the sun strike the meter as this likely will result in unacceptable under-exposure. Bracketing exposures is advisable.

One of the most effective ways of controlling contrast in landscape photographs that incorporate a portion of the sky at any time of the day is to use a graduated neutral density filter. As the sky portion of the scene is usually much brighter than the land itself, the gray portion of the filter can be positioned against the sky to lower its intensity so that all parts of the scene fall within the exposure latitude of the film.

*LONG SHADOW ON THE SERENGETI: A cloud casts a shadow over the Serengeti plains, presented here as a featureless scene devoid of life except for a few isolated trees. This isn't the view of the Serengeti that we expect. But the dramatic emptiness of the land and sky raises provocative questions not only about the immediate fate of these plains but, in a metaphorical sense, our own place in the great scheme of things.*

The technical aspects of photographing the landscape are simple and differ little from those encountered in other areas of nature photography. As with all subjects, the challenge for the artist is to express his unique perception of life. To do this he should have a thorough understanding and control of the medium; he should understand the psychology of human vision as it relates to two-dimensional design; and he should understand the essential nature of the subject, especially as it affects his personal reality. At some point in the development of a photographer, the logic of these fundamental considerations gives way to intuition, and it is usually then that his vision is expressed with the most clarity and passion.

*American Avocets, Texas*

*Preening white pelican*

**PRODUCED BY TERRAPIN BOOKS**

Managing Editor: Audrey Fraggalosch
Consulting Editors: Jennifer Josephy, Donald G. Bastian
Editorial Assistant: Pamela Brownell
Book Design: Klaus Tyne
Typography: Marcus Yearout, Digitype
Graphic Assembly: Vivian Reece
Color Separations: Toppan Printing Co. (S) Pte. Ltd.